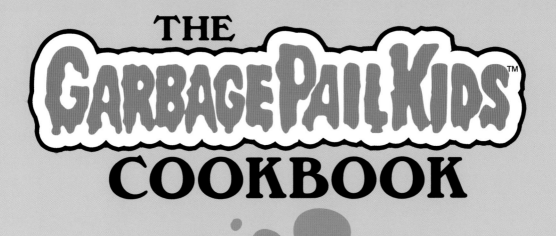

# THE GARBAGE PAIL KIDS™ COOKBOOK

## GROSS HAS NEVER BEEN SO TASTY!

**ELISABETH WEINBERG · MATT STINE**
**ILLUSTRATED BY JOE SIMKO**

**INTRODUCTION BY R.L. STINE**

**Abrams Books for Young Readers**

**New York**

**To our own Garbage Pail Kids, Devilish Dylan and Mischievous Mia. You make our lives wild, weird, messy, hilarious, and *fun*. And we love every minute of it! Well, maybe you could clean up after yourselves . . . once in a while.**

Library of Congress Control Number 2021951863

ISBN 978-1-4197-6069-3

Copyright © 2022 The Topps Company, Inc.

TM & © The Topps Company, Inc. All Rights Reserved.
Garbage Pail Kids and GPK are registered trademarks of the Topps Company, Inc.
and is officially licensed by The Topps Company, Inc.

Text by Elisabeth Weinberg and Matt Stine
Illustrations by Joe Simko
Introduction by R.L. Stine
Book design by Scott Richardson

**CREDITS FOR ORIGINAL GPK STICKERS**

**Tom Bunk:** p. 30: Saucy Sarah (All-New Series 3, 2004: 3a); p. 40: Eerie Eric (Series 3, 1986: 116a); p. 50: Pat Splat (Series 3, 1986: 89b); p. 52: Gulpin' Gabe (Series 12, 1988: 479a); p. 62: Cornelia Flake (Series 15, 1988: 587a).
**Brent Engstrom:** p. 6: Dung Beetle Baily (All-New Series 7, 2007: 18b); p. 44: Tater Todd (Food Fight!, 2021: 72b); p. 48: Magic Ian (2015 Series 1, 7a); p. 58: Doughnut Hole Joel (Food Fight!, 2021: 15a); p. 77: Sculpted Scott (All-New Series 7, 2007: 41a).
**David Gross:** p. 64: Dipping Derrick (Food Fight!, 2021: 17a).
**Joe McWilliams:** p. 68: Adam Bomb (Food Fight!, 2021: 58a).
**John Pound:** p. vi: Adam Bomb (Series 1, 1985: 8a); p. 2: Cheesy Charlie (All-New Series 1, 2003: 9a); p. 10: Nasty Nick (Series 1, 1985: 1a); p. 12: Apple Cory (Series 3, 1986: 121a); p. 16: Junkfood John (Series 1, 1985: 2a); p. 18: Luke Puke (Series 5, 1986: 170b); p. 22: New Wave Dave (Series 1, 1985: 30a); p. 24: Babbling Brooke (Series 3, 1986: 120a); p. 26: Over Flo (Series 6, 1986: 207a); p. 32: Eve Droppin' (Series 6, 1986: 240b); p. 34: Fishy Phyllis (Series 3, 1986: 108b); p. 38: Dead Ted (Series 1, 1985: 5a); p. 46: Rob Slob (Series 2, 1985: 52b); p. 54: Weird Wendy (Series 1, 1985: 16a); p. 66: Potty Scotty (Series 1, 1985: 14a); p. 70: Acne Amy (Series 2, 1985: 77b); p. 73: Brainy Janie (Series 1, 1985: 27a); p. 75: Leaky Lindsay (Series 2, 1985: 45a); p. 79: Mushy Marsha (Series 3, 1986: 101a); p. 81: Cracked Jack (Series 2, 1985: 58a); p. 83: Mad Max (Series 2, 1986: 72a).
**Joe Simko:** p. 5: Finger Lick Ken (Food Fight!, 2021: 31a); p. 36: Parma John (Brand-New Series 2, 2013: 88b); p. 60: Marsh Marlow (Brand-New Series 2, 2013: 56b).
**James Warhola:** p. 8: Walter Melon (Series 10, 1987: 405b); p. 20: Pam Ham (Series 6, 1986: 232a).

Printed and bound in China
10 9 8 7 6 5 4 3 2 1

Abrams® is a registered trademark of Harry N. Abrams, Inc.

**ABRAMS** The Art of Books
195 Broadway, New York, NY 10007
abramsbooks.com

# INTRODUCTION

## R.L. STINE

Are mealtimes scary at your house?

Kids, is the meatloaf dry and the salad wet and the potatoes lumpy and bumpy—and you don't even *know* what that gray pile is on the side of your plate?

Parents, would you describe your kids as "picky" eaters? They won't eat the chicken because there's too much skin? Someone dared put sauce on the spaghetti noodles? Two foods are touching each other on the plate, so now they're "spoiled" and can't be eaten?

My job is to make readers scream—but *not* at mealtime!

If you are a picky eater, or if you're a grownup with problem eaters, I think you may have just solved your problem. You have picked up the right book.

Here is a collection of hilarious, outrageous recipes. You will love eating these crazy creations. And just as important, you will love *creating* these dishes in the kitchen together as a family.

This is an activity book. It's a recipe book. And it's a million-laughs book. And, you will discover, the book has a very big secret.

Picky eaters will eat up the food—as well as the yucky humor.

For the past couple of years, I've been cooking up yucky humor in a book series I've been writing about the Garbage Pail Kids. In my books, Brainy Janie, Adam Bomb, Luke Puke, and a bunch of other kids live together in the town of Smellville, in a big house with no parents in sight. Their motto: "We're not bad kids. We just don't know any better."

Yes, the kids are ghastly. They are rude, lazy, sloppy, ignorant, wacky, confused, loud, and downright weird. Which, of course, is why generations of kids love them so much.

And it's why eating like a Garbage Pail Kid is so appealing.

Why not start out with a few of my favorite dishes? Herd the family into the kitchen, collect the simple and simply ridiculous ingredients, and start to whip up your next meal.

How about Luke Puke's Hurling Hummus Holes? Hard to resist—and healthy! Or maybe start out with Over Flo's Dirty Diapers? Sure, it sounds disgusting. What did you expect from the Garbage Pail Kids? But trust me, you won't be able to eat just one.

As a scary guy, my favorite item is Eerie Eric's Howlin' Hand Meatloaf. Yes, meatloaf shaped as a terrifying monster hand. How much fun will you have molding meat into a monster shape? You'll completely forget that it's actually just meatloaf!

Pam Ham's Stuffed Brain Bundles is another gross favorite of mine. Brains never tasted so good. And while you're at it, try Saucey Sarah's Sloppy Spaghetti Sliders to go with it. Or maybe Dead Ted's Maggot Chili. Another gruesome but wholesome winner.

You'll have a lot of fun preparing these rude and revolting foods. And, believe me, you'll be eating like Garbage Pail Kids in no time.

Now, here's the big secret to this book: The food looks like something from a horror movie—but *the dishes are all delicious*.

They were dreamed up by Elisabeth Weinberg, a New York City chef and a *Chopped* Champion on the Food Network, and her husband, Matt Stine (who happens to be my son), a devoted GPK fan from back in the day. Recently, Matt found a tattered box in a closet that contained his Garbage Pail Kids card collection from the '80s. The old stickers brought him a lot of memories—and are the real inspiration for this book.

Once the recipes were written, Chef Elisabeth prepared them all and fed the results to her family. Not only did we survive, but we all agreed the crazy foods she and Matt concocted are tasty and terrific. And even the pickiest eaters came back for seconds!

So go ahead. Dig in. Have fun in the kitchen—and at the table. And please—save me a few of Nasty Nick's Garlic Snots!

# PREFACE

## ADAM BOMB

Hi, my name is Adam Bomb. I'm a Garbage Pail Kid and I love to cook!

I have a total *blast* when I'm in the kitchen. I can really set the place on *fire*. When smoke explodes from the top of my head like a mushroom cloud, it even looks like I'm wearing a chef's hat!

I live in a house in Smellville with my other Garbage Pail Kid friends. When we're not getting into trouble at school or making paper airplanes out of boogers, we all like to blow off some steam by cooking up a *storm*.

At the end of the day, it looks like a bomb exploded in our kitchen. I'm talking eggs on the windows, sauce on the walls, and meatballs rolling around on the floor. We've got so many dirty dishes piled up in the sink, you can climb them all the way up to the ceiling!

We're not bad kids. We just don't know any better. We even remember to clean up after ourselves . . . once in a while! Rob Slob licks all the pots and pans until they're almost spotless. Luke Puke hurls on the counters and then wipes them down so you can barely see any chunks. And Potty Scotty grabs a toilet brush and mops the floor with buckets of water from the toilet bowl. Sometimes he even flushes the toilet *before* he fills the buckets! When our cleaning crew is done, the kitchen looks as good as new. (Well, new for a Garbage Pail Kid!)

One day, Pat Splat was smashing up a batch of his Flat 'n' Smashed Griddlers, and Dead Ted was adding the final maggot to his Maggot Chili. I stepped over a pile of half-eaten pizza crusts and thought to myself: Why should *we* be the only ones having this much fun in the kitchen? If only there were a Garbage Pail Kid cookbook . . . every kid could learn to cook and eat like we do!

I asked my best friend, Brainy Janie, what she thought. Brainy Janie is the smartest person I know. She can count all the way to ten without even needing to use her fingers! If Janie liked my idea, then it must be a good one!

Brainy Janie was so excited about the cookbook, she said she'd include a whole section of her favorite food science experiments. Janie is a brilliant scientist, so of course I said yes!

I got right to work collecting the weirdest, grossest, and coolest recipes from all my Garbage Pail Kid friends. There were so many to choose from, but these are my favorites—and I hope they will be yours, too. I guarantee you'll be *exploding* with excitement in no time!

Are you ready to cook? Roll up your sleeves, dig in, and have some *fun*—the Garbage Pail Kids way!

Barf Appétit!

# HANDY SANDY'S
# HELPFUL HINTS

If you want to cook something and you want it done right, then call me, Handy Sandy. I'm so handy in the kitchen I can cook with my eyes closed. I don't bother with recipes. I just throw some stuff in the oven and when the smoke alarm goes off, I know it's ready!

I can break a dozen eggs with my lucky hammer and start scrambling them before the pan is on the stove! My omelets are a little crunchy, but picking out bits of shell is part of the fun.

Not everyone can be as handy as me, so when you're ready to roll up your sleeves and start cooking, you gotta be extra careful and follow all the rules. That's how you make sure everything comes out just right. Trust me, you don't want to end up setting your apron on fire or supergluing a spatula to your hair. I learned that the hard way. (But at least I always know where to find my spatula!)

Take my advice and follow these handy tips for having fun and playing it safe in the kitchen. You'll be cooking like a Garbage Pail Kid in no time!

# SAFETY TIPS

 Always have an adult by your side when you're cooking in the kitchen, especially if you need to use knives, the oven, stove, blender, or mixer. The rest of the time, you can have the grownups set the table and leave you alone!

 Wash your hands with soap and water before you get started—unless you're Rob Slob. Then you should take two baths and a shower . . . 'cause you stink!

 If you have long hair, pull it back. You don't want it to catch on fire or wind up in your food. It's no fun picking hairs out of your Howlin' Hand Meatloaf during dinner!

Read through the whole recipe, and have all your ingredients and equipment ready. That way there are no surprises. Imagine getting to the last step of your Maggot Chili and realizing you forgot the maggots!

## TOOLS YOU WILL NEED

### EQUIPMENT

box grater

cutting board, knife

vegetable peeler

measuring cups/ spoons

mixing bowls (various sizes)

mixing spoons, spatula, whisk

### PANS for frying, sautéing, or cooking on a stove top.

small = 8 inches (20 cm)

medium = 10 inches (25 cm)

large = 12 inches (30.5 cm)

### POT for cooking liquid, such as boiling water or sauces.

### BAKING SHEETS

rimmed, 9 by 13 inches (23 by 33 cm)

baking dishes (assorted sizes)

# GLOSSARY OF COOKING TERMS

 **BOIL AND SIMMER:** Boiling liquid should have lots of big bubbles, with the stove on medium-high to high heat. A simmer is a gentle boil that has fewer and smaller bubbles, with the stove on lower heat.

 **CHOP:** Use a knife to cut your ingredients into pieces. Keep your hands away from the blade—you don't want any fingertips getting into your onions!

> Chopped = larger pieces, about ¼–½ inch (6–12 mm)
> Finely chopped = very small pieces, about ⅛ inch (3 mm)
> Minced = super tiny pieces, about ¹⁄₁₆ inch (2 mm)

 **KNEAD:** Use your hands to stretch, fold, and push ingredients until they come together into a solid mass, like a ball of dough.

 **SEASON TO TASTE:** Do you like your food as salty as sea water, like Fishy Phyllis? Or are you like Adam Bomb and pour in enough pepper to set your mouth on fire? Everyone has different tastes, so we're gonna leave the seasoning up to you. Add just the right amount of salt and pepper so it's exactly the way you like it!

 **SHRED OR GRATE:** Use the large holes of a box grater to shred ingredients into thin strips. Use the smallest holes of a box grater, or a food processor, to grate ingredients into a more powdery consistency.

 **SLICE:** Cut your ingredients into long or short pieces or chunks.

 **WHISK:** Use a whisk to stir or beat ingredients until completely mixed together.

---

# EXPLANATION OF MEASUREMENTS

 **HEAPING OR SCANT:** Heaping means a little more than an exact measurement. Scant means a little less.

**PACK:** Firmly push brown sugar down into your measuring cup so it's packed in tighter than Gulpin Gabe's mouth after he stuffs his face with 150 hot dogs.

**PINCH:** Use your thumb and index finger to grab a tiny amount of an ingredient, equivalent to about ¹⁄₁₆ of a teaspoon.

---

# STAPLES AND SUPPLIES

All-purpose flour              Nonstick cooking spray
Aluminum foil                  Parchment paper
Canola or vegetable oil        Salt and pepper
Extra virgin olive oil         Unsalted butter

# SPEW-WORTHY SNACKS

# CHEESY CHARLIE'S
# PIZZA SNOTCORN

GARBAGE PAIL KIDS®

CHEESY CHARLIE

When Adam Bomb asked me to create a recipe for his cookbook, of course I thought of my three favorite foods: pizza, popcorn, and boogers. My puke and pepperoni pie is a real winner. Then there's the tangy toe jam popcorn, or my spicy snot soufflé . . .

How could I decide when they're all so *good*?

That's when the recipe for Pizza Snotcorn was born! It combines all my favorite foods tossed together and baked into a crunchy, pizza-flavored, gooey, snot snack!

## INGREDIENTS - Serves 3–4

- ❏ 6 tablespoons unsalted butter, melted
- ❏ 1 teaspoon tomato paste
- ❏ ½ teaspoon dried oregano
- ❏ ½ teaspoon dried basil
- ❏ ½ teaspoon garlic powder
- ❏ 1 teaspoon salt
- ❏ Green food coloring
- ❏ 8 cups (64 g) popped popcorn
- ❏ ¼ cup (25 g) grated parmesan cheese
- ❏ ¼ cup (30 g) shredded mozzarella cheese

# STEPS

**1** Preheat the oven to 350°F (175°C). Line a baking sheet with foil.

**2** Stir together the melted butter, tomato paste, oregano, basil, garlic powder, and salt. Mix in 10 drops of green food coloring. Voilà . . . snot butter!

**3** Put the popcorn in a large bowl and add the *snot* butter, mixing well so it looks nice and snotty. This is *snot*corn, after all!

**4** Transfer the snotcorn to the prepared baking sheet, spreading it out evenly. Bake for 8 minutes, then remove from the oven and sprinkle with the two cheeses. Bake for another 4–5 minutes, until the cheese is melted. Scrape snotcorn off the baking sheet and into a serving bowl.

See what I mean? Pizza, popcorn, and boogers . . . it's the perfect combo!

**ADAM BOMB'S TIP**

We always like to line our baking sheets with foil to make clean-up nice and easy!

# FINGER LICK KEN'S
# FINGER DIPPERS

GARBAGE PAIL KIDS®

FINGER LICK KEN

This drippy dip has five layers of sloppy deliciousness. I pile on salsa, refried beans, and guacamole, and dump cheddar cheese on top. Then I stick my fingers in there and smother them in glorious glop. That's what I call finger-licking good!

Some kids don't like to get their hands dirty. Sad. So I'll do you a favor and let you lick *my* gloppy fingers. Dip as many Finger Dipper breadsticks as you like. Get 'em good and gooey, then lick 'em clean!

DO NOT TRY THIS AT HOME

## INGREDIENTS - Serves 4

### FOR THE GLOP

- ☐ 1 (16-ounce/454-g) can refried beans
- ☐ 2 tablespoons whole milk
- ☐ 8 ounces (230 g) cream cheese, at room temperature
- ☐ ½ cup (120 ml) sour cream or nonfat plain Greek yogurt
- ☐ 1 tablespoon taco seasoning
- ☐ 1 cup (240 ml) guacamole

- ☐ 1 cup (250 ml) salsa, drained of excess liquid
- ☐ 1 cup (115 g) shredded cheddar cheese

### FOR THE FINGER DIPPERS

- ☐ 1 egg
- ☐ 1 tablespoon water
- ☐ 8–10 ounces (220–280 g) pizza dough
- ☐ 12 sliced or whole raw almonds (for the fingernails)
- ☐ Salt to taste

# STEPS

## FOR THE GLOP

1. Get an 8-inch (20-cm) square baking dish or a 9-inch (23-cm) deep-dish glass pie plate. A glass pan will allow you to see all those sloppy glop layers!

2. Mix the refried beans with the milk in a small bowl until smooth.

3. In a separate bowl, mix the cream cheese with the sour cream or yogurt and taco seasoning.

4. Spread the refried bean mixture on the bottom of the baking dish. Top with the cream cheese mixture, guacamole, and then the salsa, spreading each layer evenly. Sprinkle with the cheese and admire your glorious glop. Think you can resist dipping your fingers in it?

5. Refrigerate for at least an hour, or for up to one day.

# STEPS

## FOR THE FINGERS

1. Preheat the oven to 425°F (220°C). Line a baking sheet with parchment paper.

2. Whisk the egg and water in a small bowl.

3. Tear the dough into 12 equal balls. Roll the balls into 5-inch (12-cm) "fingers."

4. Transfer the fingers to the baking sheet, spaced 1 inch (2.5 cm) apart. Brush with the egg mixture and sprinkle with salt. Firmly press an almond nail into the top of each finger. Those sure look tasty! Didn't I say I'd lend you a *hand*?

5. Bake for about 10 minutes, until golden brown.

**Start dipping those fingers, and make sure to get 'em good and gloppy!**

# DUNG BEETLE BAILY'S
# TASTY TURDS

Grandpa Baily used to say, "Don't yuck someone's yum." In Italy, they eat a cheese called *Casu marzu* which has live maggots squirming around in it. In Cambodia, they chow down on fried tarantula on a stick. And if you're a dung beetle like me, there's nothing finer than a dry-aged pile of poo.

Munching on manure may not sound yummy to you, but I'll bet these scrumptious bites of peanut butter, oats, and raisins will change your mind. I guarantee they'll be the tastiest turds you've ever had!

## INGREDIENTS - Makes 12–13 peanut butter bites

- ❏ ½ cup (120 ml) peanut butter
- ❏ 3 tablespoons honey
- ❏ ¼ teaspoon vanilla extract
- ❏ Pinch of ground cinnamon
- ❏ 1 cup (90 g) rolled oats
- ❏ ½ cup (75 g) raisins or dried cranberries
- ❏ ¼ cup (45 g) mini chocolate chips (optional)

# STEPS

**1** Mix together the peanut butter, honey, vanilla, and cinnamon in a large bowl.

**2** Stir in the oats, raisins or cranberries, and chocolate chips, if using (but *everything* is better with chocolate!). You may need to use your hands to mix it up, that's one chunky dough!

**3** Take a heaping tablespoon of dough and roll it into a ball. Repeat with the remaining dough. Chill for 30 minutes before serving.

**ADAM BOMB'S TIP**

Use a wooden skewer to turn these bites into turds on a stick!

# WALTER MELON'S

# MOLDY MELON FRIES

GARBAGE PAIL KIDS®

WALTER MELON

Most people don't know I'm a terrible chef. Like the time I tried to make spaghetti—who knew you were supposed to cook the pasta *before* adding the sauce? I never found those four cracked teeth, but Grandma Melon's old dentures really came in handy fixing my smile.

Luckily, this recipe is so easy that even *I* can make it! I cut watermelon into "fries," then leave them out for a while 'till they're extra juicy and marvelously moldy. Mold adds a tangy zip, but it takes time to grow those fuzzy spores! If you can't wait to dig in, try crushed pistachios instead. They're not quite as funky, but they'll still make your fries look deliciously rancid!

## INGREDIENTS - Serves 4–6

❏ 1 cup (240 ml) nonfat Greek yogurt
❏ 2 tablespoons honey
❏ Juice of 2 limes

❏ 1 seedless watermelon
❏ 1 cup (115 g) shelled pistachios, finely chopped

# STEPS

**1** Mix together the yogurt, honey, and juice of 1 lime. Refrigerate until ready to serve.

**2** Cut the watermelon in half. Slice it into 1-inch (2.5-cm) thick wedges and remove the rind (unless you're like me, and the rind is your favorite part. Then you should leave it on for some extra crunch!).

**3** Cut the wedges into rectangles, about 4 inches (10 cm) long and ½ inch (12 mm) thick. Then slice them into ½-inch (12-mm) thick "fries."

**4** Squeeze the juice of the second lime over the fries. Pucker up, those babies are sour!

**5** Spread the chopped pistachios on a plate. Roll the melon fries in the pistachios to coat on all sides. Now they look good and moldy, just how I like it!

**6** Serve the fries with the yogurt dip on the side.

**ADAM BOMB'S TIP**

You can turn any type of melon into a Moldy Melon Fry! Try making these with cantaloupe or honeydew!

# NASTY NICK'S
# GARLIC SNOTS

GARBAGE PAIL KIDS®

NASTY **NICK**

Most vampires want to bite your neck, but I prefer to sink my teeth ... *up your nose.* Drinking *blood*? Gross. I never touch the red stuff. But I could live forever off delicious, slimy green snot!

I've been making these Garlic Snots for centuries. I twist pizza dough into knots, brush them with garlic butter, and bake them till they're as golden brown as a Transylvanian sunset. I dunk the knots in a gooey green cheese sauce that is to *un-die* for.

What, you thought vampires couldn't eat garlic? Between you and me, it does make us a little gassy. Well, maybe a *lot* gassy. But trust me, these are worth it.

## INGREDIENTS - Makes 25 garlic knots

### FOR THE GARLIC SNOTS

- ❑ 4 tablespoons unsalted butter, melted
- ❑ 4 cloves garlic, minced; or 1 teaspoon garlic powder
- ❑ Pinch of salt
- ❑ 8–10 ounces (220-280 g) pizza dough

### FOR THE CHEESE SAUCE

- ❑ 5 tablespoons unsalted butter
- ❑ ¼ cup (30 g) all-purpose flour
- ❑ 1¼ cups (300 ml) whole milk
- ❑ 1 cup (115 g) shredded cheddar cheese
- ❑ Green food coloring
- ❑ Salt and pepper to taste

# STEPS

## FOR THE SNOTS

1. Preheat the oven to 400°F (205°C). Line a baking sheet with parchment paper. Don't have parchment paper? Borrow some from your *mummy*!

2. Mix the melted butter with the garlic and a pinch of salt.

3. Divide the pizza dough in half. Roll each half into a log about 12 inches (30.5 cm) long and 1 inch (2.5 cm) wide. Slice into 1-inch (2.5-cm) thick pieces. Roll the pieces into ropes, about ¼ inch (6 mm) thick and 5 inches (12 cm) long. Tie the ropes into knots.

4. Place the knots on the baking sheet, spaced about 1 inch (2.5 cm) apart. Brush with the garlic butter. Reserve remaining butter.

5. Bake for 12–14 minutes, until golden brown. Remove from the oven and brush with the reserved garlic butter.

# STEPS

## FOR THE CHEESE SAUCE

1. Melt the butter in a medium pot over medium heat. Add all the flour and cook for about 2 minutes, whisking constantly, until light golden brown.

2. Continue whisking and slowly pour in the milk. Continue to cook for 3–4 minutes, stirring often, until thickened.

3. Turn off the heat and stir in the cheese, whisking until smooth. Add 5 drops of food coloring and season to taste with salt and pepper. Now your sauce is a perfect shade of snot!

4. Pour the snot sauce into a bowl and dip your knots in the snot!

Tasty, right? Who needs blood when you can sink your teeth into a delicious snotty snack!

# APPLE CORY'S
# SQUIRMY WORMY SALSA WITH CINNAMON CHIPS

GARBAGE PAIL KIDS®

APPLE **CORY**

I'll never forget the first time I found a worm in my apple. I plucked it out and popped it in my mouth. The way it squirmed around as it slid down my throat . . . well, from that day on, I was hooked.

With these jiggly gelatin worms, I can enjoy my favorite snack anytime. And now you can too! Worms go great with just about anything, but I love to toss them into this fruity squirmy salsa with crunchy cinnamon chips. Make sure you get a worm in every bite, so you can really enjoy those delectable dirt-digging wrigglers.

If it ain't wormy, it ain't worthy.

## INGREDIENTS - Serves 4

**FOR THE WORMS**
(Note: Start worms at least 10 hours in advance, or up to 2 days before serving)

- ❑ 2 (3-ounce/85-g) packages raspberry gelatin powder
- ❑ 3 (¼-ounce/7-g) packages unflavored gelatin
- ❑ 3 cups (720 ml) boiling water
- ❑ ¾ cup (180 ml) heavy cream
- ❑ 15 drops green food coloring
- ❑ 100 bendy straws
- ❑ 4-cup (1-liter) container large enough to hold all the straws, about same height as straws when fully extended

**FOR THE CINNAMON CHIPS**

- ❑ 2 whole pitas

- ❑ 1 teaspoon ground cinnamon
- ❑ 2 teaspoons granulated sugar
- ❑ 2 tablespoons unsalted butter, melted

**FOR THE SALSA**

- ❑ 1 large apple
- ❑ Juice of ½ a lemon
- ❑ 1 cup (approx. 250 g) prepared worms
- ❑ ½ cup (75 g) green or red seedless grapes, cut into quarters
- ❑ ½ cup (85 g) strawberries, chopped
- ❑ ½ cup (75 g) blueberries
- ❑ ½ cup (120 ml) nonfat Greek yogurt
- ❑ 2 tablespoons honey
- ❑ Juice of 1 lime

# STEPS

## FOR THE WORMS

**1** Combine the two gelatins in a mixing bowl. Add boiling water and stir until the gelatin is dissolved. Let cool for about 20 minutes, until lukewarm. Add the heavy cream and food coloring and stir to combine.

**2** Extend the straws to their full length and place in the 4-cup (1-liter) container with the bendable part facing down.

**3** Pour the gelatin mixture over the tops of the straws until the straws are surrounded by the liquid and the container is filled almost to the top. Chill at least 8 hours.

**4** Now let's dig up some worms! Line a baking sheet with parchment paper. Remove one straw from the container. Pinch the top of the straw and run your fingers down to squeeze the worm out of the bottom. Lay the worm on the baking sheet. Repeat with the remaining worms.

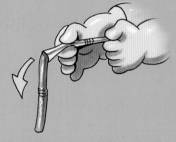

**5** Refrigerate the worms for an hour before adding to your salsa. If you can't resist, grab a worm and sneak a taste! Isn't it great how it squirms down your throat?

# STEPS

## FOR THE CINNAMON PITA CHIPS

**1** Preheat the oven to 350°F (175°C). Line a baking sheet with foil.

**2** Cut each pita into 8 triangles and place in a mixing bowl. Toss the pita with the cinnamon, sugar, and melted butter.

**3** Lay the pita on the baking sheet in a single layer. Bake for 15-20 minutes, until browned and crispy.

# STEPS

## FOR THE SALSA

**1** Peel, core, and finely chop the apple. Toss with lemon juice in a medium serving bowl.

**2** Chop half your worms into bite-sized pieces. Reserve the remaining whole worms. You can never have too many squirming around!

**3** Mix the apples with the chopped worms, grapes, strawberries, blueberries, yogurt, honey, and lime juice.

**4** Scatter the remaining whole worms over the salsa. Serve with cinnamon pita chips on the side.

**Make sure you get a worm in every bite!**

 **ADAM BOMB'S TIP**

For a real *burst* of flavor, add chopped worms to some of your other favorite GPK recipes, like Junkfood John's Junk Food Sandwich (page 16), Dipping Derrick's Double-Dipper Dips (page 64), or even Rob Slob's Garbage Pail Salad (page 46)!

# LOSE-YOUR-
# LUNCH
# LUNCHES

# JUNKFOOD JOHN'S

## JUNK FOOD SANDWICH

GARBAGE PAIL KIDS®

JUNKFOOD JOHN

Some people like to eat gross, healthy things like seaweed salad and alfalfa sprout smoothies. Yuck! Don't make me barf. Junkfood John doesn't *do* healthy.

I put the "un" in "unhealthy." I'll turn any snack into a junk food lover's dream! Like my lip-smacking, junky-to-the-max Junk Food Sandwich. I take a regular old grilled cheese, then pile on the salty potato chips, add maple syrup, and fry it in *extra* butter.

When it comes to loading up a Junk Food Sandwich, the possibilities are endless. Check out some of my add-ons to really junk it up!

## INGREDIENTS - Makes 1 sandwich

- ❏ 2 slices American or cheddar cheese
- ❏ 2 slices white bread
- ❏ ½ cup (20 g) potato chips
- ❏ 1 teaspoon maple syrup
- ❏ 4 tablespoons unsalted butter, divided

# STEPS

1 Place both slices of cheese on one slice of bread. Scatter the potato chips over the cheese. Drizzle with maple syrup. Now that's what I call junking-it-up!

2 Top with the second slice of bread and gently press down to break up the chips.

3 Melt 2 tablespoons of butter in a small nonstick pan over medium heat. Add the Junk Food Sandwich and cook for about 3 minutes, until golden brown. Flip the sandwich, add the remaining butter and cook for another 3–4 minutes, until golden brown on the other side. Remove from the pan, cool 5 minutes, then cut in half.

## Extra Junky Add-Ons:

Salty junk: pretzels, cheese puffs, popcorn

Sweet junk: chocolate chips, chopped-up candy bars, marshmallow creme, Apple Cory's Squirmy Worms (page 12)

Isn't that so much better than a seaweed salad?

# LUKE PUKE'S
# HURLING HUMMUS HOLES

GARBAGE PAIL KIDS®

LUKE **PUKE**

Luke Puke here, a.k.a. the Sultan of Spew. I'm like a walking vomit volcano: you never know when I'm gonna blow . . . chunks, that is. I guess that's why everyone's always wearing raincoats when I'm around.

You better stand back, 'cause nothing gets me gagging like these Hurling Hummus Holes. They're so good, I barf them up just so I can eat them twice! The creamy chickpea and basil filling looks so much like my own revolting regurgitations that sometimes I can't tell if it came from my stomach or the kitchen!

## INGREDIENTS - Serves 4

- ❑ 1 (15.5-ounce/439-g) can chickpeas, drained and rinsed
- ❑ Juice of 1 lemon
- ❑ ¼ cup (60 ml) tahini
- ❑ ¼ cup (40 g) chopped, frozen spinach, thawed and squeezed of excess liquid
- ❑ 2 tablespoons chopped fresh basil
- ❑ 2 tablespoons extra virgin olive oil
- ❑ Salt to taste
- ❑ ¼ cup (35 g) cooked peas
- ❑ 4 mini pitas

**1** Puree the chickpeas, lemon juice, tahini, spinach, and basil in a food processor. Drizzle in the oil and pulse to combine. Season to taste with salt.

**2** Transfer the mixture to a bowl and stir in the peas. Now your Hurling Hummus is extra chunky. Just like the real thing!

**3** Cut the tops off the pitas and stuff with heaps of that tasty upchuck, dividing evenly.

**Remember: The more you eat, the more you can bring back up for round two!**

# PAM HAM'S
# STUFFED BRAIN BUNDLES

GARBAGE PAIL KIDS®

PAM HAM

I'm Pam Ham and I'm not ashamed to say it: I swoon for swine. I binge on bundles of bacon, munch on the curly tail, slurp on the squishy nose. I go totally hog wild for every last bit of those adorable little oinkers!

The best part of the piggy is the creamy, pink brains. Have you ever had scrambled boar brains? No? Well, you don't know what you're missing.

I stuff these Brain Bundles with eggs that look just like delectable brains and then roll the "brains" in juicy slices of heavenly ham. It's a gloriously gluttonous dream come true.

Are you ready to *pig* out?

## INGREDIENTS - Serves 4

- ❏ 8 large eggs
- ❏ 6 drops red food coloring
- ❏ 2 tablespoons unsalted butter
- ❏ ½ cup (55 g) shredded cheddar cheese
- ❏ Salt and pepper to taste
- ❏ 8 slices thinly sliced ham

**1** Preheat the broiler. Take out a 9 by 13 inch (23 by 33 cm) baking dish.

**2** Crack the eggs into a large bowl, add the food coloring, and whisk to combine. Now your eggs are the color of yummy pink brains!

**3** Melt the butter in a medium nonstick pan over medium heat. Pour the "brains" into the skillet and cook for 3 minutes, stirring occasionally.

**4** Add the cheese and continue stirring for an additional 2–3 minutes, until the brains are fully cooked and the cheese is melted. Turn off the heat. Season to taste with salt and pepper. Mmmmm . . . scrambled brains.

**5** Place one slice of ham in the baking dish. Lay a second slice in the middle of the first, so they overlap.

**6** Spoon a ½ cup (110 g) of the prepared brains on one end of the ham, leaving a 1-inch (2.5-cm) border around the bottom and sides. Fold in the sides and roll the ham tightly over the brains to create a mouthwatering brain bundle. Move the bundle to one side of the baking dish, placing it seam side down. Repeat with the remaining ham and brains.

**7** Broil the ham for about 5 minutes, until lightly browned. Remove from the oven, let cool a little, and then *pig* out!

# NEW WAVE DAVE'S
# PUNKED-UP PINWHEELS

GARBAGE PAIL KIDS®

NEW WAVE DAVE

I got a thing for spray paint. Every night I throw on my leather jacket, spike up my hair, and paint the streets of Smellville. I usually stick to walls, but one time I got my hands on Mrs. Hooping-Koff's cat, Fluffy! Ever seen a rainbow cat? Totally awesome.

When I'm not spraying cats, I'm in the kitchen breaking out my can ... of spray *cheese*! I paint the wraps for these Punked-Up Pinwheels, then pile on a rad rainbow of veggies, add a slice of turkey, and roll 'em up tight.

Are you cool enough to rock these roll-ups? Shake up the spray cheese and get punky!

## INGREDIENTS - Serves 4

- ❏ 2 (8-inch/20-cm) wraps (white, whole wheat, sun-dried tomato, or spinach)
- ❏ 1 can spray cheese
- ❏ ½ red bell pepper, cut into thin strips
- ❏ ½ yellow bell pepper, cut into thin strips
- ❏ 1 medium carrot, peeled and shredded
- ❏ 1 cup (20 g) baby spinach
- ❏ 4 slices thinly sliced turkey breast

# STEPS

**1** Lay the wraps out and use the spray cheese to paint the wraps. Can you write your name in cheese? How about a cheesy self-portrait? When you're done creating your artistic masterpiece, spray a ring around the inside border of the wrap to help seal the pinwheel when it's time to roll.

**2** Arrange a row of peppers and carrots on one half of each wrap. Place the spinach on the veggies, dividing evenly, then top with two slices of turkey per wrap.

**3** Tightly roll the wraps and transfer to a cutting board, seam side down. Cut crosswise into 8 Punked-Up Pinwheels!

## ADAM BOMB'S TIP

Try making cool patterns with your veggies to really show off your *explosive* edible art skills!

# BABBLING BROOKE'S

# BB&J

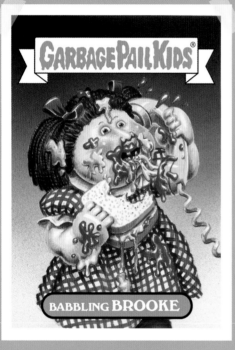

**GARBAGE PAIL KIDS**®

**BABBLING BROOKE**

My friend Dead Ted is such a good listener. Last night, I was babbling for hours about my awesome, never-before-eaten sandwich ideas. Beef liver and cheese, goat tails and cheese, chicken liver and cheese... When the convo turned to sardine melts, he stuffed worms in his ears and crawled back into his grave!

Ted rose back up just in time to hear about my BB&J! I said my Banana, Bacon & Jelly sandwich was so good, he'd never want a lame-o PB&J again. He was so excited about it, his head rolled off!

I can't wait to hear what you think. Take a bite and give me a call—we can talk all about it!

## INGREDIENTS - Makes 1 sandwich

- ☐ 2 slices of bacon
- ☐ ½ of a ripe banana
- ☐ 2 slices bread (sourdough, white or whole wheat)
- ☐ 2 tablespoons strawberry or grape jelly
- ☐ 4 tablespoons unsalted butter, divided

# STEPS

**1** Preheat the oven to 400°F (205°C). Line a baking sheet with foil.

**2** Lay the bacon out on the prepared baking sheet. Bake for 12–14 minutes, until browned and crispy. Drain on paper towels. When it's cool enough to handle, break the bacon slices in half, so there is a total of 4 pieces.

**3** Slice the banana into disks, about ¼ inch (6 mm) thick. Mmmm . . . bananas and bacon. This is making me *hungry*!

**4** Spread the jelly on one slice of bread. Add a layer of sliced banana and then the bacon. Top with the remaining slice of bread.

**5** Melt 2 tablespoons of butter in a small nonstick pan over medium heat. Cook the BB&J for 3–4 minutes, until golden brown. Carefully turn over, add the remaining 2 tablespoons of butter to the pan, and cook 3–4 minutes more, until golden brown on the other side.

**6** Remove the sandwich from the pan and let cool a few minutes before cutting in half and chowing down.

I'll bet you have a lot to say about how good this BB&J is! I know I do!

# OVER FLO'S
# DIRTY DIAPERS

GARBAGE PAIL KIDS®

OVER FLO

Pee-yew! What is that *smell*?

Oh wait, that's me.

Some people think it's gross to walk around with a fully loaded dirty diaper. Sure, my only friends are flies, and I've gotten a rash or two in my day. But I don't care. Nobody's gonna change me!

I like my diapers dirty all the time, but you don't have to soil yourself to make these tasty treats. The beefy, cheesy filling looks like a messy number two—only without the poo! I know they'll make you appreciate the stench of success!

## INGREDIENTS - Serves 4

❑ 3 tablespoons extra virgin olive oil

❑ ½ cup (65 g) finely chopped onion

❑ ½ pound (225 g) ground beef

❑ Pinch of garlic powder

❑ 2 tablespoons ketchup

❑ Salt and pepper to taste

❑ 4 slices American cheese

❑ 1 (8-ounce/226-g) can refrigerated crescent roll dough

# STEPS

1. Preheat the oven to 350°F (175°C). Line a baking sheet with parchment paper.

2. Heat the oil in a medium pan over medium-low heat. Add the onion and cook for 8–10 minutes, stirring occasionally, until softened.

3. Increase the heat to medium. Add the ground beef and garlic powder. Cook 3–4 minutes more, stirring to break up the beef, until it's nice and brown, like the color of you-know-what! Turn off the heat.

**4** Mix in the ketchup and season to taste with salt and pepper. Transfer to a bowl and set aside to cool for 20 minutes.

**5** Cut each square of cheese diagonally to make 4 triangles, for a total of 16 slices.

**6** Unroll the crescent dough. Pull the dough triangles apart and cut each in half to make 2 smaller triangles, for a total of 16 diapers.

**7** Now let's get those diapers *dirty*! Lay a slice of cheese on each diaper. Spoon 1 tablespoon of poop—I mean beef—over the cheese.

**8** Fold the 3 points of the diaper over the beef. Gently press the ends to seal. Place on the baking sheet, spaced 1 inch (2.5 cm) apart. Bake for 12–14 minutes, until golden brown.

## Take a whiff! Don't those Dirty Diapers smell so delicious?

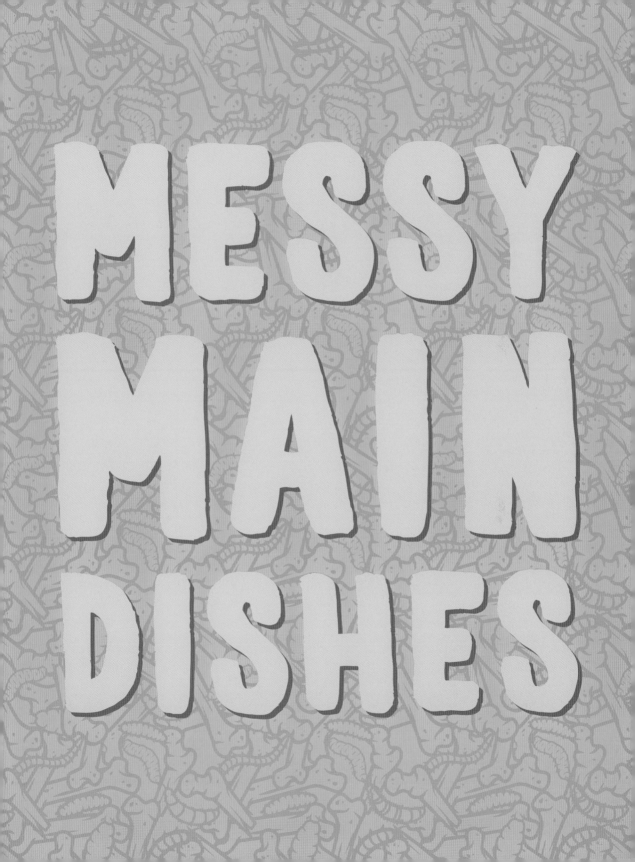

# MESSY MAIN DISHES

# SAUCEY SARAH'S
# SLOPPY SPAGHETTI SLIDERS

GARBAGE PAIL KIDS®

SAUCEY SARAH

I love sauce so much, I once filled a pool with a thick and chunky meat sauce and swam in it all summer. After three months of blazing sun, the meat got a little overcooked, but the mold kept it nice and moist.

When it comes to sauce, too much is never enough. These Sloppy Spaghetti Sliders are especially good with three-month-old moldy meat sauce, but if you don't have any lying around, a tasty marinara will do the trick. Dump on as much of that saucy goodness as you can. The sloppier, the better!

If you don't have sauce dripping from your eyebrows, you didn't do it right.

## INGREDIENTS - Serves 4

- ❏ ½ pound (227 g) spaghetti, broken into small pieces
- ❏ 1–1½ cups (240–360 ml) marinara sauce, depending on how saucy you want to get
- ❏ ¼ cup (10 g) chopped fresh basil
- ❏ Salt and pepper to taste
- ❏ 4 tablespoons unsalted butter, melted
- ❏ ½ teaspoon garlic powder
- ❏ 12 slider buns
- ❏ ½ cup (55 g) shredded mozzarella cheese
- ❏ 2 tablespoons grated parmesan cheese

# STEPS

1 Preheat the oven to 350°F (175°C). Take out a 9 by 13 inch (23 by 33 cm) baking dish.

2 Cook the spaghetti according to the package directions in boiling, salted water. Drain and toss with the marinara sauce and basil. Season to taste with salt and pepper. (Throw in some moldy meat sauce, if you're lucky enough to have some lying around!)

3 Mix the butter with the garlic powder and set it aside.

4 Lay the bottom halves of the buns in the baking dish. Top each with a big spoonful of that extra-saucy spaghetti. Did sauce splatter on your face? Good for you, now you're getting the hang of it!

5 Sprinkle the mozzarella and parmesan over the spaghetti, then add the top halves of the buns. Brush the tops of the buns with the melted butter mixture.

6 Bake for 10 minutes, until the cheese is melted and the buns are lightly toasted. Use a spatula to scoop out the sliders.

**Take a big, sloppy, super-saucy bite!**

# EVE DROPPIN'S
# WAX 'N' CHEESE

My ears are so big, I can hear a Himalayan housefly pass gas somewhere on Mount Everest. Jealous? I know, it *is* pretty cool.

When your ears are the size of an elephant's, the earwax oozes out by the gallon. It's *super* fun to play with. But you know what's even better than playing with my gooey green wax? Eating it!

I take all that extra gunk, mix it with spinach and cheese, and whip up my delicious Wax 'n' Cheese! Don't have enough wax to spare? No worries, the sauce is still good without it! I pour the sauce over orecchiette, or "little ears" pasta. Yeah, you *heard* that right. Pasta shaped like ears! How awesome is *that*?

## INGREDIENTS - Serves 8 as a side dish, 4 as a main course

- ❑ 1 (16-ounce/453-g) box orecchiette ("little ears" pasta)
- ❑ 5 tablespoons unsalted butter
- ❑ ¼ cup (30 g) all-purpose flour
- ❑ 3 cups (720 ml) whole milk
- ❑ Salt and pepper to taste
- ❑ ¼ cup (60 ml) sour cream
- ❑ 2 cups (230 g) shredded cheddar cheese
- ❑ 1 (10-ounce/283-g) box frozen, chopped spinach, thawed and squeezed of excess liquid

# STEPS

1 Cook the pasta according to the package directions in boiling, salted water. Drain and transfer to a large serving bowl.

2 Melt the butter in a medium pot over medium heat. Add all the flour and cook for about 2 minutes, whisking constantly, until light golden brown.

3 Continue whisking and slowly pour in the milk. Cook at a gentle simmer for 8–10 minutes, stirring frequently, until thickened and smooth. Turn off the heat and season to taste with salt and pepper.

4 Add the sour cream, cheddar cheese, and spinach. Mix until the sauce is smooth and creamy. (If you've got extra wax, now's the time to stir it in!)

5 Pour the sauce over the pasta and stir to combine.

Isn't that Wax 'n' Cheese sooo delicious? Tell me what you think—I'm all *ears*!

# FISHY PHYLLIS'S
# FRYING PAN SIZZLERS

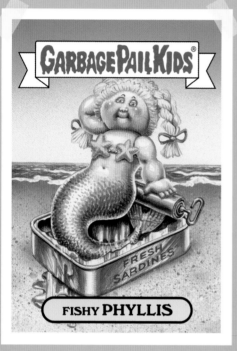

GARBAGE PAIL KIDS®

FRESH SARDINES

FISHY **PHYLLIS**

There are a lot of things that may surprise you about mermaids. Like, did you know that we are really *gross*? We take baths in whale blubber. We use squid guts for toothpaste. And we absolutely stink. Like dead-fish-that's-been-rotting-in-the-sun-for-three-weeks-kind of stink.

We don't just smell like rotten fish. We *eat* rotten fish! And the stinkier the better. I use rancid tuna belly to make my awesome Frying Pan Sizzlers. Canned tuna will work in a pinch, but the sizzlers won't have the same stench. I mix in eggs, mayo, mustard, and spices, and then fry 'em up into putrid tuna-tastic croquettes.

Ready to eat like a real mermaid? Well, let's get fishy!

## INGREDIENTS - Serves 4

- ❏ 2 (5-ounce/142-g) cans albacore tuna in water, drained
- ❏ 1 teaspoon Dijon mustard
- ❏ 2 teaspoons mayonnaise
- ❏ ¼ teaspoon onion powder
- ❏ 1 large egg, beaten
- ❏ Juice of ½ a lemon
- ❏ ½ cup (50 g) plain bread crumbs, divided
- ❏ Salt and pepper to taste
- ❏ 1 cup (240 ml) extra virgin olive oil or canola oil, for frying

# STEPS

**1** Use a fork to mash up the canned tuna (or rancid tuna belly!) in a medium bowl. Add the mustard, mayonnaise, onion powder, eggs, lemon juice, and a ¼ cup (25 g) of the bread crumbs. Season to taste with salt and pepper and mix to combine.

**2** Scoop out a ¼ cup (60 g) of the tuna mixture, roll it into a ball, and gently flatten into a thick fishy patty. Repeat to make 8 total. *Oooh-weee*, those patties really *stink*!

**3** Put the remaining ¼ cup (25 g) bread crumbs on a plate and roll the patties in the bread crumbs, coating on all sides.

**4** Heat the oil in a large pan over medium heat. Fry the patties for 3–4 minutes, until golden brown. Look at those sizzlers sizzle! Flip the patties and cook for another 3–4 minutes, until golden brown on the other side. Remove from the pan and drain on paper towels.

**Whaddya think? Don't you love eating like a mermaid? I hope those sizzlers are *extra* fishy!**

# MAMMA MIA QUESO-DILLA

I love cheese on everything. I even like my jokes cheesy.

How do you get a mouse to smile?
*Say cheese!*

What's a dog's favorite cheese?
*Mutts-a-rella!*

What cheese is so smart it can change a lightbulb?
*Cheese Whiz!*

You want more? Or is that *Gouda-nuff* for you? Nothing is *cheddar* than a *grate* joke, but I'm as serious as an aged Gorgonzola when it comes to this Mamma Mia Queso-dilla. *Brie-lieve* me, it is *seriously* delicious. I spoon marinara sauce on a tortilla, add slices of roasted eggplant and *extra* cheese, and cook till it's golden and crispy. *Hole-y* cow, this is the eggplant parm-quesadilla combo that cheesy dreams are made of!

## INGREDIENTS - Serves 4

- ❑ 1 medium eggplant, approximately 2 pounds (910 g), thinly sliced (about 1/8 inch/3 mm thick)
- ❑ 1 tablespoon salt
- ❑ 4 tablespoons extra virgin olive oil
- ❑ 1/2 cup (120 ml) marinara sauce
- ❑ 4 (8-inch/20-cm) flour tortillas
- ❑ 1/2 cup (55 g) shredded mozzarella cheese
- ❑ 2 tablespoons grated parmesan cheese
- ❑ 6 tablespoons unsalted butter, divided

# STEPS

**1** Preheat the oven to 400°F (205°C). Line 2 baking sheets with foil.

**2** In a colander, toss the sliced eggplant with salt and set aside to drain for 30 minutes.

**3** Squeeze the eggplant to remove excess liquid. Lay it out in a single layer on the prepared baking sheets, dividing the slices evenly. Drizzle oil over the eggplant, then bake for 18–20 minutes, until the eggplant is cooked through and lightly browned.

**4** Spread the marinara sauce on 2 tortillas. Sprinkle each with the mozzarella and parmesan, then add a layer of eggplant. Top with the remaining tortillas. Just in *queso* you didn't know, this is gonna be so good it'll blow your *rind*!

**5** Melt 2 tablespoons of butter in a medium nonstick pan over medium heat. Cook first queso-dilla for 3–4 minutes, until golden brown. Flip over, add an additional tablespoon of butter, and cook 3–4 minutes more, until golden brown on the other side. Remove from the pan and drain on paper towels. Repeat with second 'dilla, using the remaining 3 tablespoons butter.

**6** Time to *cut the cheese!* Slice each queso-dilla into 8 triangles before serving.

Mamma mia, I love the smell of cheese wafting through *Gruyère*! I just *ricotta* take a bite or I'm gonna *melt*!

# DEAD TED'S
# MAGGOT CHILI

*BRAINS! BRAAAINS!*
That's all us zombies ever eat. Brain butter, brain burgers, brain bourguignon, brain-battered biscuits . . . YUCK!

I'm more of a down-to-earth kind of guy. Plants, bugs, dirt, worms . . . I'll grab anything that's crawling around my casket when I rise from the grave.

That's why I came up with this recipe for vegetarian Maggot Chili. It's chock-full of beans and veggies and topped with a handful of maggots. Deliciously brain-free, just how I like it. Don't panic if you can't find any maggots in your grave. Any bug or worm will do—you can even use some maggoty-looking pasta if that's all you can dig up!

## INGREDIENTS - Serves 4

- ❏ 2 tablespoons extra virgin olive oil
- ❏ 1 cup (110 g) chopped yellow onion
- ❏ ½ cup (50 g) chopped celery
- ❏ 1 cup (140 g) chopped carrot
- ❏ ½ cup (75 g) chopped red or green bell pepper
- ❏ Salt and pepper to taste
- ❏ 2 cloves garlic, chopped
- ❏ 1 teaspoon chili powder
- ❏ 1 teaspoon ground cumin
- ❏ 1 teaspoon paprika

- ❏ 1 teaspoon dried oregano
- ❏ 1 cup (145 g) cooked corn kernels
- ❏ 1 (28-ounce/793-g) can diced tomatoes, with juices
- ❏ 1 (15-ounce/425-g) can black beans, drained and rinsed
- ❏ 1 (15-ounce/425-g) can pinto beans, drained and rinsed
- ❏ 2 cups (480 ml) vegetable stock or water
- ❏ ½ cup (70 g) orzo, cooked according to package directions (about ¼ cup/42 g uncooked), for maggot garnish

# STEPS

**1** Heat the oil in a large pot over medium heat. Add the onion, pepper, carrot, celery, and a pinch of salt. Cook for 8–10 minutes, stirring occasionally, until veggies are softened.

**2** Add the garlic and spices and cook for 1 minute, stirring constantly.

**3** Add the corn, tomatoes, beans, and vegetable stock or water. Stir to combine and bring to a simmer. Cook at a gentle simmer for 30–35 minutes, until most of the liquid is absorbed. Season to taste with salt and pepper.

**4** Spoon the chili into bowls. Top with a handful of orzo (or maggots if you found any!) and *dig* in!

**Now doesn't that look so much tastier than a bowl full of brains?**

## ADAM BOMB'S TIP

If you prefer a gluten-free maggot meal, substitute cooked white rice for the orzo!

39

# EERIE ERIC'S
# HOWLIN' HAND MEATLOAF

GARBAGE PAIL KIDS®

EERIE ERIC

I'm usually a nice kid, except when I turn into a howling beast with monster hands and razor-sharp claws. My friends started saying stuff like, "I don't think we can hang out anymore. I've only got nine fingers left and I'd like to keep it that way." Or, "It's not you, it's me. I've got a thing about full body hair."

I get it. You don't want to get too close to someone who may bite your head off at the first sign of a waxing gibbous.

But are you brave enough to try my Howlin' Hand Meatloaf? It's shaped like my monster claws in the light of a full moon. If you'd rather cook dinner than *be* dinner, this is the recipe for you!

## INGREDIENTS - Serves 4

- ❏ 2 tablespoons extra virgin olive oil
- ❏ 2 cups (250 g) chopped yellow onion, plus five 1 by 1 inch (2.5 by 2.5 cm) slices of onion for fingernails
- ❏ ¼ teaspoon dried thyme
- ❏ ¼ cup (60 ml) chicken stock
- ❏ 2 tablespoons Worcestershire sauce

- ❏ 1 tablespoon tomato paste
- ❏ 2 pounds (910 g) ground beef
- ❏ ½ cup (50 g) plain breadcrumbs
- ❏ 2 large eggs, beaten
- ❏ ⅓ cup (75 ml) ketchup
- ❏ Salt and pepper to taste

# STEPS

1 Preheat the oven to 325°F (165°C). Line a baking sheet with foil.

2 Heat the oil in a medium pan over medium-low heat. Add the chopped onions and thyme. Cook for 10–12 minutes, stirring occasionally, until the onions are softened. Turn off the heat and add the stock, Worcestershire sauce, and tomato paste. Let cool for 10 minutes.

3 Combine the beef, onion mixture, bread crumbs, and eggs in a large bowl. Season to taste with salt and pepper and mix well. Transfer to the prepared baking sheet.

AWOOOoo...

**4** Are you feeling brave? Shape the beef mixture into a monster hand about 1½ inches (4 cm) thick and 11 inches (28 cm) long, with 1-inch (2.5-cm) thick fingers spaced slightly apart. Spread the ketchup over the entire hand. Press the reserved onion slices on the tips of the fingers, for the fingernails. Are you howling at the moon yet? Owwooooo!

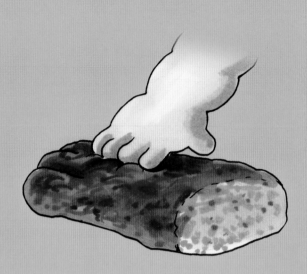

**5** Bake for approximately 45 minutes, until the hand is firm and an internal thermometer registers 165°F (75°C). Set aside to cool for 10 minutes before digging in.

That is, if you dare . . .

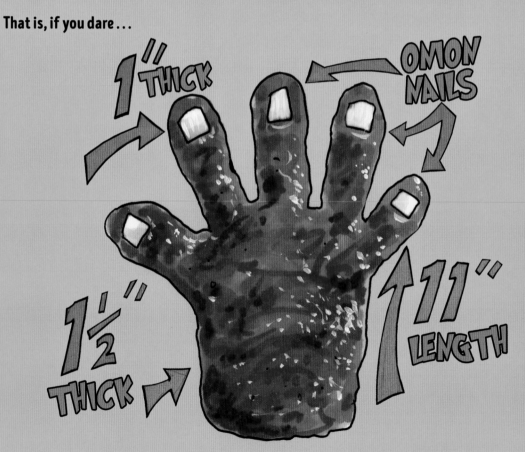

1" THICK

OMON NAILS

1½" THICK

11" LENGTH

# STOMACH-TURNING SIDES

# TATER TODD'S
# CHOCOLATE SPUDS AND BUGS

GARBAGE PAIL KIDS®

TATER TODD

I was peeling potatoes when a slippery spud shot out of my hands and knocked over my entire colony of black ants! They swarmed over a chocolate cake and onto a tray of steaming baked potatoes. What a mess!

But I wasn't gonna waste a perfectly good dinner ... and that's when I discovered the delicious combo of Chocolate Spuds and Bugs!

What, you've never had chocolate on a potato? Take it from someone who knows a thing or two about taters: it's totally *tuber-riffic*! Ants add extra crunch to these cheesy twice-baked spuds, but chocolate sprinkles work in a pinch. They look like ants, taste like chocolate, and won't try to crawl off your plate.

## INGREDIENTS - Makes 8 twice-baked potato halves

- ❏ 4 russet potatoes
- ❏ 2 tablespoons extra virgin olive oil
- ❏ 8 tablespoons or 1 stick unsalted butter, at room temperature
- ❏ ½ cup (120 ml) sour cream or plain Greek yogurt
- ❏ ½ cup (55 g) shredded cheddar cheese
- ❏ 2 tablespoons whole milk
- ❏ Salt and pepper to taste
- ❏ 4 teaspoons chocolate sprinkles

# STEPS

1. Preheat the oven to 350°F (175°C). Line a baking sheet with foil.

2. Wash the potatoes, then rub the skins with oil. Place the potatoes on the prepared baking sheet and bake for about 1 hour, turning once halfway through, until completely tender when pierced with a knife. Set aside to cool slightly.

3. Mix the butter with the sour cream in a medium bowl.

4. Cut each potato in half lengthwise. Scoop out the insides and add to the bowl with the butter and sour cream. Be careful not to tear the skin. I like my taters picture perfect! Place the scooped shells back on the baking sheet.

5. Smash the scooped potato with the butter and sour cream until smooth. Stir in the cheese and milk and season to taste with salt and pepper. Spoon the mixture into the potato shells so it comes just over the top. Return to the oven and bake for 15 minutes, until warmed through.

6. Scatter a ½ teaspoon of chocolate sprinkles over each potato before serving. (If you see any ants crawling around your kitchen counter, add them for a little extra crunch!)

**ADAM BOMB'S TIP**

Add more or less sprinkles depending on how chocolaty you like your taters!

45

# ROB SLOB'S
# GARBAGE PAIL SALAD

GARBAGE PAIL KIDS®

ROB SLOB

You can toss just about anything into a Garbage Pail Salad. A hunk of old cheddar cheese, a half-eaten head of wilted lettuce, that last bite of salami your dog licked but was too good to throw away . . . Chop it up, toss it all together with one of my signature dressings, and chow down!

Last week I made some for Saucey Sarah, and she ran out of the room screaming, *"What's that smell?!"*

If you'd rather let your dog have the salami and you can't find any moldy cheese in your sock drawer, give this recipe a try. It'll be the finest gourmet garbage you've ever had!

## INGREDIENTS - Serves 4

### FOR THE GARBAGE PAIL SALAD

- ❑ 2 cups (110 g) chopped romaine or iceberg lettuce
- ❑ ½ cup (100 g) chopped salami, ham, chicken, or turkey
- ❑ 1 cup (110 g) chopped mozzarella or cheddar cheese
- ❑ 2 hard-boiled eggs, chopped
- ❑ 1 cup (135 g) grape tomatoes, sliced in half
- ❑ 1 cup (133 g) chopped cucumber
- ❑ 4–6 olives, pitted and chopped
- ❑ 1 cup (145 g) cooked corn
- ❑ ½ cup (75 g) dried cranberries or raisins

### FOR ROT-YOUR-TEETH VINAIGRETTE

- ❑ 2 tablespoons maple syrup

- ❑ 2 tablespoons balsamic vinegar
- ❑ 1 teaspoon Dijon mustard
- ❑ ½ teaspoon salt
- ❑ ½ cup (120 ml) extra virgin olive oil

### FOR ROTTENEST RANCH DRESSING

- ❑ ½ cup (120 ml) whole milk
- ❑ 2 teaspoons lemon juice
- ❑ ½ cup (120 ml) mayonnaise
- ❑ ½ cup (120 ml) nonfat plain Greek yogurt
- ❑ 1 teaspoon garlic powder
- ❑ ½ teaspoon onion powder
- ❑ 1 teaspoon chopped chives
- ❑ ¼ teaspoon salt

## STEPS

### For the Garbage Pail Salad

1 Mix all the ingredients together and toss with one of Rob Slob's Garbage Salad Dressings.

## STEPS

### For Rot-Your-Teeth Vinaigrette

1 Combine the maple syrup, vinegar, mustard, and salt in a bowl.

2 Slowly whisk in the oil until the mixture is thick and creamy.

## STEPS

### For Rottenest Ranch Dressing

1 Combine the milk and lemon juice in a small bowl and let sit for 5 minutes.

2 In a separate bowl, whisk together the mayonnaise, yogurt, garlic powder, onion powder, chives, and salt. Whisk in the whole milk mixture and stir until smooth. Extra dressing can be kept in the refrigerator for up to 3 days.

I hope you found some special garbage to toss into your salad, like the mystery meat in the back of your fridge or an extra brown overripe banana. Remember: When in doubt, don't throw it out . . . toss it *in*!

# MAGIC IAN'S
# MAGICAL MYSTERY CASSEROLE

**GARBAGE PAIL KIDS**®

MAGIC IAN

Sure, I've heard of Houdini. But did Houdini ever saw a chicken in half and then put it back together? Well, maybe I put the chicken's butt where the head was supposed to be—but at least it could still lay eggs!

Did Houdini ever create a pasta dish . . . without the pasta? That's my greatest trick of all. And now I'm passing my secrets along to you! Using nothing but a fork, I turn squash into spaghetti, then toss it with a mystifying ricotta cheese sauce. After one bite you'll be saying, "How did he *do* that?"

Behold the wonder of the great Magic Ian's Magical Mystery Casserole!

## INGREDIENTS - Serves 8

- ☐ 1 (3½- to 4-pound/1.6-to 1.8-kg) spaghetti squash
- ☐ 2 tablespoons extra virgin olive oil
- ☐ Salt and pepper to taste
- ☐ 3 tablespoons unsalted butter
- ☐ 2 cloves garlic, minced

- ☐ 2 tablespoons all-purpose flour
- ☐ 1 cup (240 ml) chicken or vegetable stock
- ☐ ½ cup (120 ml) heavy cream or whole milk
- ☐ ½ cup (125 g) ricotta cheese
- ☐ ½ cup (50 g) grated parmesan cheese
- ☐ ½ cup (20 g) chopped fresh basil

# STEPS

1. Preheat the oven to 400°F (205°C). Line a baking sheet with foil. Take out a 9 by 13 inch (23 by 33 cm) baking dish.

2. Cut the squash in half lengthwise. Scoop out the seeds. Drizzle the oil over the insides and season with salt and pepper.

3. Place the squash cut side down on the prepared baking sheet and poke holes in the skin with a fork. Bake for 30–40 minutes, until tender when pierced with a knife. Set aside to cool. Turn the oven down to 350°F (175°C).

4. Drag a fork along the inside of the squash, creating spaghetti-like strands. Abracadabra, squash is now pasta! Take that, Houdini!

5. Melt the butter in a medium pot over medium heat. Add the garlic and flour and cook for about 2 minutes, whisking constantly, until the flour is light golden brown.

6. Whisk in the stock and heavy cream or milk. Bring the mixture to a simmer and cook for 5–6 minutes, stirring often, until thickened. Turn off the heat, stir in the ricotta and parmesan cheese, and the squash strands. Season to taste with salt and pepper.

7. Transfer the squash mixture to the baking dish. Cook in the oven for 15–20 minutes, until heated through. Sprinkle with the chopped basil before serving.

And remember, a magician never tells his secrets, so let's keep this one between us, OK?

**ADAM BOMB'S TIP**

Substitute cooked spaghetti for the squash. It may not be a *mind-blowing* magic trick, but it'll still taste great!

# PAT SPLAT'S
# FLAT 'N' SMASHED GRIDDLERS

GARBAGE PAIL KIDS®

PAT SPLAT

Things are always falling on me. Like the time a box of rotten zucchini landed on my head and splattered all over the floor. I slipped on a squished squash and stumbled right into a bunch of sticky fly traps. It took me three hours to pull the glue off my eyebrows and pick the flies out of my teeth.

But the flattened zucchini on the bottom of my shoe gave me a great idea . . . pancakes! I ran home to scrape the squash off my sneakers. Then I whipped up a tasty batter and fried up a batch of these delicious Flat 'n' Smashed Griddlers!

## INGREDIENTS - Serves 4

- ❏ 1 pound (455 g) zucchini
- ❏ 3 tablespoons minced scallions
- ❏ 2 large eggs, beaten
- ❏ ½ cup (65 g) plus 1 tablespoon all-purpose flour
- ❏ 1 teaspoon baking powder
- ❏ ¼ cup (25 g) grated parmesan cheese
- ❏ 1 teaspoon salt
- ❏ ½ teaspoon dried oregano, thyme, parsley, or basil
- ❏ 1 cup (240 ml) canola oil, for frying

# STEPS

**1** In a large bowl, grate the zucchini using the large holes of a box grater. Mix in the scallions, eggs, flour, baking powder, parmesan, salt, and dried herbs. (If there's any squished zucchini stuck to the bottom of your shoe, add that too!)

**2** Heat the oil in a medium pan over medium heat. Scoop out a ¼ cup (60 ml) of the zucchini batter and drop it carefully into the pan. Cook for 3–4 minutes, until golden brown. Flip, then cook for 3–4 minutes more, until golden brown on the other side. Drain on paper towels and repeat with the remaining batter. (Griddlers can be warmed in a 300°F/150°C oven before serving.)

Aren't those griddlers great? Now when something delicious falls on your head, you know what to do: pick up the pieces, and get cooking!

# GULPIN' GABE'S
# FACE STUFFERS

GARBAGE PAIL KIDS®

GULPIN' GABE

Nobody can beat me in an eating contest. I hold the world record for most fish sticks ever consumed— three hundred in ten minutes flat (my burps smelled like cod for three days!) One time, I ate 150 hot dogs in five minutes. I could've eaten more, but they ran out of buns.

I love being number one, but it's not always as fun as it sounds. When you eat 150 hot dogs you get sick. *Real sick.* Ever barfed up 150 wieners? They don't taste as good on the way back up. And if I see another fish stick, I'm gonna hurl. Again.

You may be tempted to shovel these maple-glazed sweet potato Face Stuffers in your mouth by the handful. Trust me, don't overdo it. They're a lot better on your plate than in your toilet.

## INGREDIENTS - Serves 4

- ❑ 2 pounds (910 g) sweet potatoes, peeled and cut into 1-inch (2.5-cm) chunks
- ❑ 2 tablespoons unsalted butter, at room temperature
- ❑ 2 tablespoons maple syrup
- ❑ Salt to taste

# STEPS

**1** Preheat the oven to 350°F (175°C). Take out a 9 by 13 inch (23 by 33 cm) baking dish.

**2** Place the sweet potatoes in a single layer in the baking dish. Add the butter and maple syrup and mix to combine. Season to taste with salt.

**3** Cover the dish with foil. Bake for 50–60 minutes, until the potatoes are cooked through and easily pierced with a knife. Remove the foil and continue roasting for about 10 minutes, until the Face Stuffers are lightly browned. Allow to cool for a bit before serving.

One time I shoveled a handful of hot stuffers in my mouth and I couldn't feel my tongue for a week! I still won the Million Meatball challenge, but it wasn't easy!

# WEIRD WENDY'S
# CREEPY CAULDRON STEW

WEIRD WENDY

We witches go batty for broccoli. And you should too! Broccoli is a *super*food, and it gives you magical superpowers. If you eat enough broccoli, you'll be able to turn your pet newt into a porcupine! Or teach your dog how to do your homework!

My Creepy Cauldron Stew is a bubbling brew of creamy broccoli that's brimming with brocco-licious *super*power. It's so good, it'll knock you right off your broomstick.

But don't forget the eyeballs! I always like to have a few bobbing around. I usually keep a jar of pickled peepers in my pantry, but if you're running low, try my squishy cheesy eyeballs instead!

## INGREDIENTS - Serves 4

### FOR THE CHEESY EYEBALLS
(can be prepared up to 1 day in advance)

- ❑ 4 ounces (115 g) cream cheese, at room temperature
- ❑ ½ cup (55 g) shredded cheddar cheese
- ❑ Pinch of garlic powder
- ❑ Pinch of dried oregano
- ❑ Vegetable oil or nonstick cooking spray, for greasing your hands
- ❑ 8 blueberries

### FOR THE CREEPY CAULDRON STEW

- ❑ 1 pound (455 g) broccoli
- ❑ 2 tablespoons unsalted butter
- ❑ ½ cup (65 g) chopped yellow onion
- ❑ 1 cup (240 ml) water
- ❑ 1 teaspoon fresh thyme or ¼ teaspoon dried thyme
- ❑ ¼ cup (60 ml) sour cream
- ❑ Salt and pepper to taste

# STEPS

## FOR THE EYEBALLS

**1** Put the cream cheese, cheddar cheese, and spices in a bowl and mix until smooth.

**2** Grease your hands with the oil or nonstick cooking spray. Scoop out 2 tablespoons of the cheese mixture and roll into a 1-inch (2.5-cm) ball. Repeat, for a total of 8 eyeballs.

**3** Gently press a blueberry into the center of each eyeball. Jeepers creepers check out those peepers! Set the eyeballs aside while you make the stew, or store in the refrigerator for up to 1 day.

# STEPS

## FOR CREEPY CAULDRON STEW

1 Chop the broccoli into small florets.

2 Melt the butter in a large pan over medium heat. Add the onions and cook for 3–4 minutes, until softened. Toss in the broccoli, thyme, and water. Reduce the heat to low, cover the pan, and cook for 12–15 minutes more, until the broccoli is completely tender when pierced with a fork. Double, trouble, broccoli bubble . . . let's turn this brew into Cauldron Stew!

3 Transfer the broccoli mixture to a food processor. Add the sour cream, season to taste with salt and pepper, and pulse until mostly smooth. Spoon into a serving bowl and top with the eyeballs.

Grab a spoon, dig into an eyeball, and start waving your magic wand! What brocco-superpowered spell will you cast first?

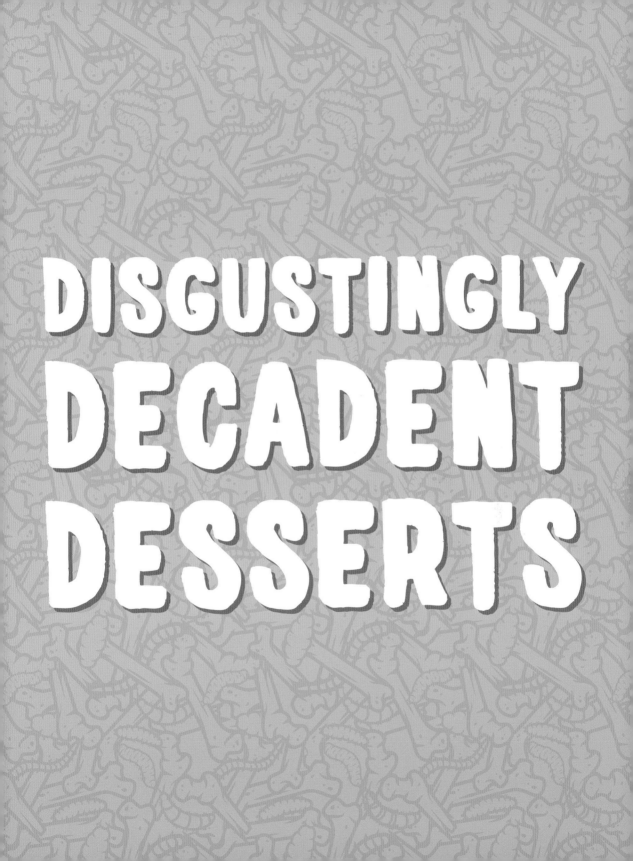

# DISGUSTINGLY DECADENT DESSERTS

# DOUGHNUT HOLE JOEL'S
# DOUGHMUFFS

GARBAGE PAIL KIDS®

DOUGHNUT HOLE JOEL

When Gulpin' Gabe challenged me to a muffin-eating competition, I stuffed a doughnut hole in his ear and said it was doughnuts or bust! Then it occurred to me . . . Why not eat *both*? And so, the Doughmuff was born.

Part doughnut, part muffin, these poppable little pastries are impossible to resist. I take it one delicious Doughmuff at a time, but Gabe loves them so much, he once ate thirty in under a minute. That kid never learns. He ended up barfing Doughmuffs all over my shoes! What a waste.

## INGREDIENTS - Makes 36 Doughmuffs

### FOR THE DOUGHMUFFS

- ❏ Nonstick cooking spray, for greasing the muffin tins
- ❏ 1½ cups (190 g) all-purpose flour
- ❏ 1 teaspoon ground cinnamon
- ❏ ¼ teaspoon ground nutmeg
- ❏ 1 teaspoon baking powder
- ❏ ½ teaspoon baking soda
- ❏ Pinch of salt
- ❏ ½ cup (120 ml) canola oil

- ❏ ½ cup (100 g) granulated sugar
- ❏ ½ cup (110 g) packed light brown sugar
- ❏ 1 large egg
- ❏ 1 teaspoon vanilla extract
- ❏ ¾ cup (180 ml) plain yogurt

### FOR THE TOPPING

- ❏ 4 tablespoons unsalted butter
- ❏ ½ cup (100 g) granulated sugar
- ❏ 2 teaspoons ground cinnamon

# STEPS

**1** Preheat the oven to 350°F (175°C). Grease three 12-count mini muffin tins with nonstick cooking spray. Yeah, yeah, I know it's a *muffin* tin. They only *look* like muffins—got it?

**2** Combine the flour, cinnamon, nutmeg, baking powder, baking soda, and salt in a medium bowl.

**3** In a separate large bowl, whisk together the oil with both sugars, egg, and vanilla. Whisk in half the flour mixture, then all the yogurt, then the remaining flour to create a smooth batter.

**4** Spoon a heaping tablespoon of batter into each prepared muffin cup, filling each about three-quarters full.

**5** Bake the Doughmuffs for 12–15 minutes, until light golden brown and a toothpick inserted in the center comes out clean. Set aside to cool while you make the topping.

**6** To make the topping: Melt the butter. Stir together the cinnamon and sugar in a small bowl.

**7** Remove the warm Doughmuffs from the muffin tins. Generously brush the tops of the Doughmuffs with the melted butter, then roll in the cinnamon sugar, coating all sides.

Try to resist eating too many. You don't want to end up barfing them up like Gulpin' Gabe!

## ADAM BOMB'S TIP

If you don't have mini muffin tins, you can make 12 larger Doughmuffs in a standard-sized muffin tin. Use about a ¼ cup (60 ml) of batter for each muffin cup and bake them 20–25 minutes. They won't be as poppable but they'll still be impossible to resist!

# MARSH MARLOW'S
# DRIPPY S'MORES BARS

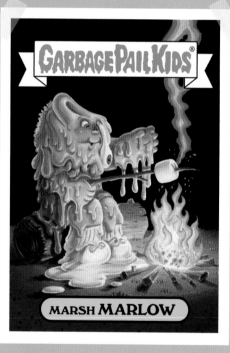

GARBAGE PAIL KIDS®

MARSH MARLOW

There's nothing like sitting around a campfire, making s'mores, and telling spooky stories. Eerie Eric once told us about a zombie deer who lived in the woods and ate the heads off bats. Luke Puke was so scared he barfed right on the fire—all over my roasting marshmallows. I ate them anyway, of course. I would never let a good marshmallow go to waste.

My gooey Drippy S'mores Bars bring back all those great memories. If I close my eyes, I can almost taste the barf. Best part is, you can make them any time of year, even if you don't have a campfire.

## INGREDIENTS - Makes 16 bars

- ❏ Nonstick cooking spray or softened butter for greasing the pan
- ❏ 5 graham crackers
- ❏ 8 tablespoons or 1 stick unsalted butter, melted and cooled slightly
- ❏ 2 large eggs
- ❏ ¾ cup (165 g) packed light brown sugar
- ❏ ¼ cup (50 g) granulated sugar
- ❏ 2 teaspoons vanilla extract
- ❏ 1 cup (125 g) all-purpose flour
- ❏ Pinch of salt
- ❏ 1½ cups (70 g) mini marshmallows
- ❏ 1 cup (175 g) semisweet chocolate chips
- ❏ ¼ cup (40 g) butterscotch chips or white chocolate chips (optional)

# STEPS

**1** Preheat the oven to 350°F (175°C). Line an 8-inch (20-cm) square baking pan with foil and grease with the nonstick cooking spray or softened butter.

**2** In a bowl, use your hands to break up the graham crackers into small pieces.

**3** In a separate, large bowl, whisk together the melted butter, eggs, both sugars, and vanilla. Add the flour and salt and mix until just combined.

**4** Using a spatula or wooden spoon, mix in the graham crackers, mini marshmallows, chocolate chips, and butterscotch chips, if using. The batter will be very thick. If you want to make these extra gooey, sneak a couple of extra marshmallows in there. That's what I would do!

**5** Spread the batter in the prepared pan. Bake for 30–35 minutes, until set in the center. Cool slightly before serving.

# CORNELIA FLAKE'S
# BOTTOM OF THE BOWL CEREAL COOKIES

CORNELIA FLAKE

The only thing I eat is cereal. For lunch, I'll have a CLT (cereal, lettuce, and tomato) sandwich with *extra* mayonnaise. It's cereal and beef stew with a side of cereal salad for dinner. I eat three boxes of cereal for breakfast, and the only bowl big enough to hold it all is our toilet!

You know that awful feeling when a box of cereal is almost empty, with just a few scraps and crumbs left behind? Well, I mix every last bit into my soft and chewy Bottom of the Bowl Cereal Cookies. Use any of your breakfast favorites to whip these chunky cookies up. You'll never waste a single flake again!

## INGREDIENTS - Makes 25 cookies

- ❏ 2½ cups (315 g) all-purpose flour
- ❏ ¾ teaspoon baking soda
- ❏ ¾ teaspoon baking powder
- ❏ ¼ teaspoon salt
- ❏ 16 tablespoons or 2 sticks unsalted butter, at room temperature
- ❏ 1 cup (200 g) granulated sugar

- ❏ 1 tablespoon packed light brown sugar
- ❏ 1 large egg
- ❏ 2 teaspoons vanilla extract
- ❏ 2½ cups (75 g) of cereal (assorted or all one kind), divided
- ❏ 1 cup (175 g) vanilla frosting

# STEPS

1. Preheat the oven to 350°F (175°C). Line 2 baking sheets with parchment paper.

2. Combine the flour, baking soda, baking powder, and salt in a bowl.

3. In a stand mixer fitted with the paddle attachment, or in a bowl with a hand mixer, cream the butter with both sugars for about 3 minutes, until light and fluffy. Add the egg and vanilla and mix another minute.

4. Reduce the mixer speed to low. Slowly add the flour mixture, then 2 cups (60 g) of cereal, mixing until just combined. Make sure you don't waste a single flake!

5. Scoop out a heaping tablespoon of dough, roll into a ball, and place it on the prepared baking sheets. Repeat with the remaining dough, leaving about a 1-inch (2.5-cm) space between the cookies.

6. Bake the cookies for 12–15 minutes, rotating once, until just set. Remove from the oven and let cool completely.

7. When the cookies are cool, frost with the icing and decorate with the remaining ½ cup (15 g) of cereal.

Cereal for breakfast, lunch, dinner, *and* dessert. It's a cereal-lover's dream come true!

# DIPPING DERRICK'S
# DOUBLE-DIPPER DIPS

GARBAGE PAIL KIDS®

DIPPING DERRICK

The only way to dip it right is to dip it twice. Maybe it's gross to take a slobbery, half-eaten chip and stick it back in the bowl, but I don't care. Gross is how I roll.

It takes just a few minutes to whip up these simple and delicious dessert dips, and start practicing your double-dipping skills. Try them with pretzels, graham crackers, chips, sliced apples, strawberries, or animal crackers. Walter Melon's Moldy Melon Fries (page 8) are also a great way to go!

Dip it, lick it, and dip it again. It's the double-dipper way!

## INGREDIENTS - Each double-dipper makes about 2 cups (480 ml)

### CHOCOLATE CHIP DOUBLE-DIPPER

- ❏ 4 ounces (115 g) cream cheese, at room temperature
- ❏ 8 tablespoons or 1 stick unsalted butter, at room temperature
- ❏ 2 teaspoons vanilla extract
- ❏ 1 cup (100 g) confectioners' sugar, sifted
- ❏ ¼ cup (55 g) packed light brown sugar
- ❏ 1 cup (175 g) semisweet chocolate chips

### STRAWBERRIES AND CREAM DOUBLE-DIPPER

- ❏ 4 ounces (115 g) cream cheese, at room temperature
- ❏ 2 (5.3-ounce/170 g) containers of strawberry yogurt
- ❏ ¼ cup (25 g) confectioners' sugar, sifted
- ❏ 1 teaspoon vanilla extract
- ❏ ½ cup (85 g) fresh strawberries, chopped

### MARSHMALLOW DOUBLE-DIPPER

- ❏ 6 ounces (175 g) cream cheese, at room temperature
- ❏ 8 ounces (170 g) marshmallow creme
- ❏ 1 teaspoon vanilla extract
- ❏ ¼ cup (50 g) rainbow sprinkles

## Chocolate Chip Double-Dipper

1 Mix cream cheese, butter, and vanilla in a medium bowl until smooth and fluffy (you can do this by hand or with a stand or handheld mixer).

2 Gradually mix in confectioners' sugar, then the brown sugar and chocolate chips. Refrigerate for about 30 minutes before double-dipping.

### ADAM BOMB'S TIP

Try using your Double-Dippers as a frosting for Acne Amy's Pimple Poppers (page 70) or Cornelia Flake's Bottom of the Bowl Cereal Cookies (page 62)! You can even spread a dipper on a bagel for a breakfast treat that's the *bomb*!

# STEPS

## Strawberries and Cream Double-Dipper

1 Mix the cream cheese in a medium bowl until smooth (you can do this by hand or with a stand or handheld mixer).

2 Add the yogurt, confectioners' sugar, and vanilla and mix again until smooth. Stir in the chopped strawberries. Refrigerate until ready to serve.

# STEPS

## Marshmallow Double-Dipper

1 Mix the cream cheese, marshmallow creme, and vanilla extract in a medium bowl until smooth and fluffy (you can do this by hand or with a stand or handheld mixer). Top with the sprinkles. Refrigerate until ready to serve.

# POTTY SCOTTY'S
# POOP COOKIES

GARBAGE PAIL KIDS®

POTTY SCOTTY

I come up with all my best ideas when I'm alone in the loo, relaxing on my porcelain throne. Like the singing toilet that played "Tinkle, Tinkle, Little Star" ... Or the prankster potty with disappearing toilet paper ... What about the toilet bowl that was also a fish tank? That one was the best! Well, until someone flushed ...

But these amazing Poop Cookies are my greatest inspiration. I roll out a chocolaty sugar cookie dough and twist it into my favorite turd-tastic shape. They look so realistic you may think twice before taking a bite! Pure potty genius!

## INGREDIENTS - Makes 25 cookies

- ❏ 1½ cups (190 g) all-purpose flour
- ❏ ¾ cup (70 g) unsweetened cocoa powder
- ❏ Pinch of salt
- ❏ 12 tablespoons or 1½ sticks unsalted butter, at room temperature

- ❏ 1¼ cups (250 g) granulated sugar
- ❏ 1 egg
- ❏ 2 teaspoons vanilla extract
- ❏ 1 teaspoon baking powder

# STEPS

1. Combine the flour, cocoa powder, and salt in a small bowl.

2. In a stand mixer fitted with the paddle attachment, or in a bowl with a hand mixer, beat the butter and sugar on high speed for 3 minutes, until light and fluffy. Add the egg and vanilla and beat 1 minute more.

3. Reduce the mixer speed to low. Add the flour mixture and mix until just combined. Isn't that the perfect hue of poo?

4. Gather the dough into a ball and wrap it in plastic wrap. Refrigerate at least 2 hours (can be prepared a day in advance).

5. Preheat the oven to 350°F (175°C). Line 2 baking sheets with parchment paper.

6. Roll 2 tablespoons of dough into a 6- to 8-inch (15- to 20-cm) snake. Coil the snake into a neat, little turd and place on the prepared baking sheet. Repeat with the remaining dough, spacing the cookies 2 inches (5 cm) apart.

7. Bake for 12–15 minutes, until set. Cool for 10 minutes before serving.

Didn't I tell you these looked just like *real* turds? I like to pile them on the kitchen counter and totally freak out my friends!

# ADAM BOMB'S
# BLENDER BLASTERS

GARBAGE PAIL KIDS®

ADAM BOMB

These *dynamite* Blender Blaster recipes are the *bomb*. They're gonna *blow* your mind—even if you don't have an exploding blender for a brain. I'm *bursting* with excitement just thinking about them.

The vanilla banana Kablooey Blaster is gonna *rock* your world. And the strawberry smoothie Volcano Blaster is *erupting* with flavor.

Can you guess my secret ingredient? It *pops* right out of your glass... You guessed it—popping candy! Are you ready to *blast* off? Well...3...2...1...*go!*

## INGREDIENTS - Makes 2 milkshakes or smoothies

### KABLOOEY BLENDER BLASTER

- ❑ 2 cups (290 g) vanilla ice cream
- ❑ ¼ cup (60 ml) whole milk
- ❑ 1 cup (240 ml) crushed ice
- ❑ 1 very ripe banana
- ❑ 4–6 tablespoons popping candy (pick your favorite colors and flavors!)

### VOLCANO BLENDER BLASTER

- ❑ 1 cup (150 g) frozen strawberries
- ❑ ¼ cup (60 ml) plain yogurt
- ❑ ½ cup (120 ml) whole milk
- ❑ 3 tablespoons honey
- ❑ 4–6 tablespoons popping candy (pick your favorite colors and flavors!)

## Kablooey Blender Blaster

1 *Blast* the ice cream, milk, ice, and banana in a blender until smooth.

2 Divide the mixture between 2 tall glasses, filling each halfway. Don't add too much or the candy will *explode* all over your kitchen! Well, that does sound kind of awesome.

3 Stir in 1 tablespoon of popping candy to each glass and stand back! It really *pops*! Top with another 1–2 tablespoons of candy for extra *zip*, then grab a straw and start slurping that blaster!

# STEPS

## Volcano Blender Blaster

1 *Blast* the strawberries, yogurt, milk, and honey in a blender until smooth.

2 Divide the mixture between 2 tall glasses, filling each halfway. Remember not to add too much!

3 Stir 1 tablespoon of popping candy into each glass and stand back! Add another 1–2 tablespoons for a super *rockin'* topper. Grab a straw and let the *fireworks* begin!

### ADAM BOMB'S TIP

Try a Blender Blaster combo with both blasters in the same glass! Start with the Volcano Blaster, and then add the Kablooey on top. And for an even bigger *bang*, throw in some extra popping candy. Like Grandma Bomb always said, "The more *explosions*, the better!"

# ACNE AMY'S
# PIMPLE POPPERS

GARBAGE PAIL KIDS®

ACNE **AMY**

Is anything better than squeezing a big, juicy pimple and watching it splatter all over the mirror? So satisfying. I'm lucky cause my face is covered in lots of luscious zits waiting to be popped! If your face is clear, have no fear. I've got acne to spare and I'm happy to share!

These dreamy Pimple Poppers are the perfect end to any meal. I take a fluffy cupcake and fill it with just enough vanilla pudding to ooze out of the top. Don't forget to give them a good squeeze!

## INGREDIENTS - Makes 16 cupcakes

- ❑ 1 (3.4-ounce/96-g) package instant vanilla pudding mix
- ❑ 1 cup (125 g) all-purpose flour
- ❑ ¼ cup (25 g) plus 2 tablespoons unsweetened cocoa powder
- ❑ ¾ teaspoon baking powder
- ❑ ½ teaspoon baking soda
- ❑ Pinch of salt
- ❑ 2 large eggs

- ❑ ¾ cup (150 g) granulated sugar
- ❑ ¼ cup (55 g) packed light brown sugar
- ❑ ⅓ cup (75 ml) canola oil
- ❑ 1 teaspoon vanilla extract
- ❑ ½ cup (120 ml) buttermilk (or ½ cup/120 ml whole milk mixed with 2 teaspoons lemon juice)
- ❑ 2 cups (350 g) chocolate frosting
- ❑ Red icing in a fine-tipped tube

# STEPS

1. Preheat the oven to 350°F (175°C). Place cupcake liners in 16 muffin tins.

2. Prepare the vanilla pudding according to the package directions. Transfer to a small resealable plastic bag. I can't wait to watch that pudding ooze out of these poppers!

3. In a large bowl, whisk together the flour, cocoa powder, baking powder, baking soda, and salt.

4. In a separate bowl, whisk together the eggs, both sugars, oil, vanilla, and buttermilk or milk with lemon. Add this mixture to the bowl with dry ingredients and whisk until just combined.

5. Pour a scant ¼ cup (60 ml) of batter into each muffin tin, filling about halfway. Don't overfill or the batter will bubble over and make a big zitty mess!

6. Bake for 18–20 minutes, until a toothpick inserted in the center comes out clean. Cool completely in the pan.

7. Remove the cupcakes from the pan and frost with the chocolate icing. Use a paring knife to cut a 1-inch (2.5-cm) wide hole out of the center of each cupcake.

8. Cut a small hole in the corner of the pudding bag. Gently squeeze the pudding into the middle of the cupcakes so it comes just to the top. Circle the pudding with a rim of red icing to complete your zit.

Now go ahead and take a bite of one of those juicy Pimple Poppers!

GARBAGE PAIL KIDS®

BRAINY JANIE

**DO NOT EAT**

It's always a good idea to play with your food, but not all food experiments are tasty enough or safe to eat. Look for the symbol above to know which experiments are good for just having fun, and *not* chowing down.

Did you know that the four basic food groups are cereal, candy bars, chicken nuggets, and boogers? Everyone knows no meal is complete without boogers, but some people forget about the chicken nuggets.

Did you know that the only cure for hiccups is to drink water through your nose with a metal straw while standing on your head and barking like a dog? Works every time!

Did you know that dinosaurs didn't eat meat? That's why they all died when a giant meatball, called a *meaty-or*, fell from the sky. There were no salad trees left to eat after that.

If you knew these food science facts, then you're a certified brainiac like me!

I've gathered some of Smellville's finest scientific minds to share their favorite foodie experiments with you. Only a true brainiac can use the magic of science to transform ordinary ingredients into stretchy edible slime, squishy dough, and even . . . ice cream!

Welcome to Brainy Janie's Food Science Lab!

# LEAKY LINDSAY'S
# EDIBLE SLIME

GARBAGE PAIL KIDS®

LEAKY LINDSAY

I've got so much snot pouring out of my nose I could fill a bathtub and still have 10 buckets to spare. I blow through forty boxes of tissues, and that's *before* breakfast.

You may think it'd be annoying to leak all the time, but I don't. I just remember what Grandma Leaky used to say: "Leaky Lindsay, when life gives you lemons, make lemonade." I take all that snot and turn it into super-fun slime! And not just any slime . . . *edible* slime!

This experiment will help you whip up your own edible slime, even without buckets of snot. So let's get slimy!

## INGREDIENTS

- ❏ 12 marshmallows
- ❏ ¼ cup (60 ml) canola or vegetable oil
- ❏ ½ cup (65 g) cornstarch

# STEPS

**1** Place the marshmallows and oil in a microwave safe bowl. Microwave for about 45 seconds, until the marshmallows are puffed. Be careful, the bowl and marshmallows will be *hot*!

**2** Add the cornstarch to the bowl and mix in with a spoon until smooth.

**3** Make sure the mixture is cool enough to handle, then get your hands in there to knead and stretch that slime! Don't forget to take a bunch of slimy bites!

## ADAM BOMB'S TIP

Add a few drops of food coloring for colorful slime or 1–2 tablespoons of chocolate syrup for chocolate slime!

# SCULPTED SCOTT'S
# SQUISH-TASTIC GPKDOUGH

SCULPTED SCOTT

I love making super-squishy GPKdough. I can squeeze it and shape it into just about anything. Like that time I molded it into a life-size model of the Smellville playground. When Pat Splat tried to climb the monkey bars, the whole thing squished down, and he fell flat on his face!

Try making lots of different colors with this GPKdough before you start shaping and molding it into whatever crazy creations you can think of! What are *you* gonna squish? Fool your friends like I did— they'll love it!

## INGREDIENTS

- ☐ 3 cups (375 g) all-purpose flour
- ☐ 1 cup (290 g) salt
- ☐ 2 tablespoons vegetable oil
- ☐ 1 cup (240 ml) water
- ☐ Food coloring, in assorted colors

# STEPS

**1** Combine the flour, salt, oil, and water in a large mixing bowl. Using your hands, mix and knead the mixture together until it comes together into a smooth dough.

**2** Divide the dough into balls. Each ball can be a different squishy color! Use your finger to make a small well in the center of each ball. Add about 10 drops of food coloring to each well. Fold the food coloring into the dough and knead until it is mixed completely.

**3** Start shaping and molding! What will you make first? Can you fool your friends with a GPKdough hamburger? What about a life-size version of Mrs. Hooping-Koff's cat, Fluffy?

# MUSHY MARSHA'S
# WACKY ICE CREAM

GARBAGE PAIL KIDS®

MUSHY MARSHA

I'm a total ice cream fanatic. I'm always coming up with ideas for awesome new flavors, such as strawberries 'n' beans, or cinnamon sardine swirl, or beef jerky and brussels sprout jubilee.

When you eat as much ice cream as I do, you learn to make it yourself. That way you always have some in your freezer! I put all my ingredients in a couple of plastic bags, add some ice and salt, and shake up my favorite frozen treat faster than you can say caramel chicken pot pie.

## INGREDIENTS - Serves 4

- ❑ 1 cup (240 ml) half-and-half
- ❑ ½ cup (100 g) granulated sugar
- ❑ 1 teaspoon vanilla extract
- ❑ ¼ cup (72 g) kosher salt
- ❑ 2 large and 1 small resealable plastic bags
- ❑ Gloves or large dishtowel

# STEPS

**1** Pour the half-and-half, vanilla, and sugar into the small resealable plastic bag. Squeeze out the excess air and seal firmly. Make sure the bag is completely sealed or you'll end up with salty ice cream!

**2** Fill 1 of the large resealable plastic bags about halfway with ice. Add the salt to the ice.

**3** Place the small plastic bag inside the large bag, on top of the ice and salt. Top with extra ice, allowing enough room to seal the large bag. Seal the bag, then place it inside the second large bag and seal. This will prevent the ice from leaking as it melts.

**4** Put your gloves on, or wrap the bags in a dishtowel. It's about to get cold in here!

**5** Shake up the bag as hard as you can for about 6 minutes. Don't bang the bag against a counter or it may break.

**6** Take out the smaller bag and rinse the outside with cold water. Wipe off the top before opening to remove any salt.

**7** Open the bag, stir the ice cream with a spoon and dig in!

## ADAM BOMB'S TIP

Try creating your own wacky flavor combos with fruit, caramel, chopped-up cookies (Potty Scotty's Poop Cookies on page 66 would be great!) . . . use your imagination! Mushy Marsha's cinnamon swirl sounds good, but maybe leave out the sardines.

# CRACKED JACK'S
# GO SUCK AN EGG

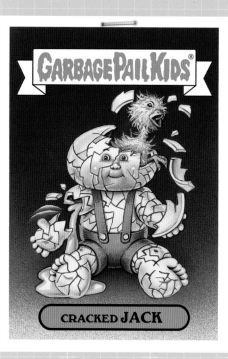

GARBAGE PAIL KIDS®

CRACKED JACK

My name wasn't always Cracked Jack. It used to be just Jack. But one day, faster than you can say *hard-boiled*, I slipped on a banana peel and fell face-first into Benedict, my pet porcupine. Well, that broke my yolk. Now everyone calls me *Cracked* Jack.

Speaking of yolks, have you ever tried to suck up an egg yolk with a plastic bottle? Think you can do it without breaking the yolk? Test your separating skills in this egg-cellent egg-speriment. Let's get cracking!

## INGREDIENTS

❏ Eggs (egg-speriment with as many as you like!)  ❏ An empty plastic bottle

# STEPS

**1** Crack an egg onto a small plate or in a bowl. Be careful not to break the yolk!

**2** Lightly squeeze the plastic bottle. Don't remove all the air.

**3** Keep squeezing the bottle and gently place the mouth of the bottle over the egg yolk, just touching the surface of the yolk. Slowly release your squeeze and watch the bottle suck up the egg yolk!

**4** Try returning the egg yolk back into the whites without breaking it! Think you can suck up *two* egg yolks at the same time?

## ADAM BOMB'S TIP

After you're done egg-sperimenting, these eggs would be *dynamite* in Pam Ham's Stuffed Brain Bundles (page 20)!

# MAD MAX'S
# MAGIC MUCK

GARBAGE PAIL KIDS®

MAD MAX

It can be kind of lonely being a mad scientist, spending all your days in a creepy lab doing crazy experiments. It's true, my only friends are a collection of preserved rat brains and petrified frog livers. But when an experiment finally bubbles over and crawls across the floor and I scream "It's alive! It's alive!," it makes everything all worthwhile.

This Magic Muck will turn you into a mad scientist, just like me! What is Magic Muck? It's a liquid and a solid at the same time! It's a slime so strong you can stomp it with your feet and so slimy it can melt between your fingers. Experiment with your muck all you want, but don't let it crawl away!

## INGREDIENTS

❑ 1¼ cups (160 g) cornstarch

❑ ½ cup (120 ml) water

# STEPS

**1** Place the cornstarch in a large bowl and add water.

**2** Use your hands to mix the cornstarch and water together and let the fun begin!

## ADAM BOMB'S TIP

Try putting different-size objects on the surface of the muck and seeing which ones sink! If you stick your hand in the muck, how long does it take you to get it out? Try making a muck ball in your hands and see how long you can hold it before it turns back into goo!!

# OUT WITH A BANG!

## ADAM BOMB

ADAM BOMB

Is your kitchen a hideous mess? Are you still scraping the egg yolk out of your hair? Are there piles of "Dirty Diapers" all over the floor? Good! Then you've successfully cooked your way through *The Garbage Pail Kids Cookbook*!

It's been a real *blast* making all these awesome gross and tasty dishes with you. I hope they were even more deliciously disgusting than you could have ever imagined! What were some of your favorites? (Well, besides my *popping* Blender Blasters, of course.)

Now that you know what it means to cook like a real Garbage Pail Kid, why don't you come on over to our house in Smellville and join us in the kitchen? We can chop together, stir together, bake together, hurl together . . . Rob Slob might even let you lick the pots and pans after we're done! I'm so excited, I'm gonna *explode*!

So whaddya say? How about you break out that snotty, saucy, cheesy, drippy, slimy, gooey, moldy, sticky, yucky, mucky, glop-stained apron and let's have some more *fun*!

Until then . . . Barf Appétit!

# ACKNOWLEDGMENTS

We are so grateful for the brilliant team of people who helped create this crazy cookbook. Thanks to Ira Friedman at Topps, for trusting us and for sharing his wisdom and expertise in all things Garbage Pail Kids. Thank you, Joe Simko, our insanely talented illustrator whose artistic genius pours out of every page!

Thanks to Charlie Kochman and Jessica Gotz at Abrams for their insight and impeccable attention to detail. And to the terrific team at Quarto, who took such great care with the book and us, especially Delia Greve, Taryn Albright, and Scott Richardson.

And of course, R.L. Stine, for all your help and guidance. And for being a good sport, even when our children act like Garbage Pail Kids.

And to all of our friends and family who bravely served as taste-testers, even when the food looked (almost) too disgusting to eat.

# ABOUT THE AUTHORS

**ELISABETH WEINBERG** is the executive chef and owner of Miss Elisabeth's Catering in New York City and a Food Network *Chopped* champion. Elisabeth and Matt also co-authored *Little Chef*, a picture book published in 2018. When she's not developing disgusting recipes, Elisabeth spends her time cooking wholesome food for her kids, most of which ends up on the floor. Luckily their new puppy, Marlo, is always standing by to clean up the mess.

**MATT STINE** is a Tony award–winning orchestrator and two-time Grammy-nominated music producer who also works as a sound designer on Broadway and Off-Broadway. When he's not in the theater, Matt helps his wife and co-author, Elisabeth, cook up ideas for grossing out children. He is so lucky to be married to someone who shares his juvenile sense of humor and love of snot, poop, and puke. Matt is not the first writer in his family. His father is Goosebumps author R.L. Stine.

# ABOUT THE ILLUSTRATOR

**JOE SIMKO** is an artist known for his happy-horror style. He is one of the premiere Garbage Pail Kids illustrators for the Topps Company and lives in New York City with his wife, son, dog, and many, many boxes of cereal.

# ABOUT THE TOPPS COMPANY

**THE TOPPS COMPANY, INC.**, originator of Garbage Pail Kids, Mars Attacks, and Bazooka Joe brands, was founded in 1938 and is the preeminent creator and marketer of physical and digital trading cards, entertainment products, and distinctive confectionery.